W9-BZB-585

ALSO BY DON GABOR:

How to Start a Conversation and Make Friends

ILLUSTRATIONS BY MARY POWER

A FIRESIDE BOOK
PUBLISHED BY SIMON & SCHUSTER INC.
NEW YORK LONDON TORONTO SYDNEY TOKYO

FIRESIDE
SIMON & SCHUSTER BUILDING
ROCKEFELLER CENTER
1230 AVENUE OF THE AMERICAS
NEW YORK, NEW YORK 10020

COPYRIGHT © 1989 BY DON GABOR

ALL RIGHTS RESERVED
INCLUDING THE RIGHT OF REPRODUCTION
IN WHOLE OR IN PART IN ANY FORM.

FIRESIDE AND COLOPHON ARE REGISTERED TRADEMARKS
OF SIMON & SCHUSTER INC.

DESIGNED BY DIANE STEVENSON / SNAP · HAUS GRAPHICS

MANUFACTURED IN THE UNITED STATES OF AMERICA

1 2 3 4 5 6 7 8 9 10

LIBRARY OF CONGRESS CATALOGING IN PUBLICATION DATA

Gabor, Don.
How to talk to the people you love / Don Gabor ;
[illustrations by Mary Power].
p.   cm.
ISBN 0-671-66196-5
1. Interpersonal communication.   2. Intimacy.   3. Friendship.
4. Communication in the family.   5. Communication in marriage.
I. Title.
BF637.C45G33   1989   89-11572
158'.2—dc20   CIP

DEDICATION

AND

ACKNOWLEDGMENTS

This book is dedicated to my family, my friends, my wife, Eileen, and our two cats, Toby and Sophie. Our intimate conversations were part of the inspiration for this book. I also want to thank Laura Yorke, my editor at Fireside, for her sharp editorial pencil, and the following people for their cooperation and suggestions:

Ruth Bachrach
Dr. Philmore Berger
Bob Bloom
Daniel Carman
Adrian Ehrlich
Julie Haynes
Andy Levine
Steve Levine

Jeannette Lofas
Jonathan Pease
Nancy Pease
Mary Power
Lucille Rhodes
Jacqueline Berger-Yudelowitz, MSW

CONTENTS

I have written *How to Talk to the People You Love* because students often ask me how to approach personal conversations with loved ones without feeling nervous about saying the wrong thing. This book is based on the premise that people often have as much or more difficulty communicating with a friend, lover, or family member than with a stranger. Expressing personal information or speaking one's mind without inducing misunderstandings or hostility requires the ability to carry on a conversation, plus much more. Intimate conversations are motivated by a compelling desire to honestly reveal emotions and thoughts; and require a desire to go beyond politeness as well as individuals' mutual trust and respect.

WHAT IS AN INTIMATE CONVERSATION?

An intimate conversation is a personal communication in which you honestly express your feelings and opinions by using your heart and your head. When you combine coolness with compassion, logic with understanding, affection with discipline, and trust with openness, you will focus on real issues while speaking assertively with common sense, insight, and love.

WHAT ARE THE BENEFITS OF INTIMATE CONVERSATION?

You can benefit from intimate conversations in at least two ways. They increase intimacy between friends and they provide greater insights into your personal relationships. When people calmly exchange their viewpoints and feelings on emotional subjects, there will be a better understanding between them, whether they are best friends, husband and wife, parent and child, or stepfamily members.

HOW CAN THIS BOOK HELP YOU?

How to Talk to the People You Love is a follow-up to *How to Start a Conversation and Make Friends,* because even good conversationalists often experience nervousness, anxiety, and misgivings when communicating with the people they know well. This book presents alternatives to holding in what you want to say or exploding into a rage that leaves emotions raw and torn.

This book presents a solid framework of tested communication techniques in a direct and easy-to-read guide that includes specific examples, tips, and motivators to help you effectively talk with the people you love.

PART 1

INTIMATE CONVERSATIONS WITH YOUR FRIENDS

BUILDING
BETTER
FRIENDSHIPS

One friend in a lifetime is much; two are many; three are hardly possible.

—Henry Adams

There are as many definitions of friendship as there are friends, but one thing is certain—most people seek someone whom they can trust and confide in. A true friend values you as a person and does not care if you wear the latest fashions, are rich, or are the chief executive officer of a large company. A friend accepts you for who and what you are without trying to change you. But making and keeping a good friend is easier said than done. The reason? Friendships are hard to make and easy to break.

Do friendships just happen? Is it chemistry that explains how two people can hit it off and become friends? Certainly individual personalities are important when two people become friends, but other factors also play a role. Since we have different needs at different stages of our lives, our friends help fill some of those requirements. For example, if you move to a new city, finding a friend helps overcome the sense of isolation and loneliness that comes from not knowing anyone. Making friends at work helps you feel like part of a team and provides an opportunity to be recognized and appreciated for a job well done.

People also become friends to share their opinions and feelings. Often we do not really know what we think and feel until we hear ourselves speak and see the reaction of the people whose opinions we value. In this way our friends help us confirm, reshape, and expand our views. They provide us with a yardstick for measuring whether our perceptions are realistic or way out in left field.

Another factor that propels us toward friendships is the fear of being alone and living in an emotional vacuum. Studies show that our biggest fear is not nuclear war, starvation, or illness. Rather, it is being alone without companionship or love. Since most of us thrive and grow on personal contact, true friendships develop from a mutual commitment with a firm foundation of trust, respect, exchange, and emotional support.

THE FRIENDSHIP TREE

*T = **TRUST***: *"Friendships, like marriages, are dependent on avoiding the unforgivable." —John D. MacDonald*

*R = **RESPECT***: *"Love your friend with his faults." —Proverb*

*E = **EXCHANGE***: *"Friendship is an arrangement by which we undertake to exchange small favors for big ones." —Baron de Montesquieu*

*E = **EMOTIONAL SUPPORT***: *"A true friend will see you through when others see that you are through." —Robert Louis Stevenson*

TRUST = CONFIDING + UNDERSTANDING

"**I** *know that I can tell my friend just about anything and trust that she will understand and keep my secrets to herself."*

When friends reveal private feelings, trust in each other grows naturally. As a result, their intimate conversations provide opportunities to monitor the emotional depth of the friendship. As the conversations become more personal, revealing, or sensitive, the trust and the relationship will continue to expand. On the other hand, if there are few personal revelations, or if one person seems to hold back, then chances are the trust in the friendship may be reaching a leveling-off point.

To increase trust in your friendship you can say:

"There is something personal that I would like to share with you."

"If you don't mind, I'd like to ask you a personal question, but feel free to not answer if you wish."

"I've never mentioned this before, but I want to tell you . . ."

"I trust you, so please keep what I am about to tell you in the strictest confidence."

True friendship based on trust allows people to be vulnerable without fear of being used or taken advantage of. Trust in a friendship takes time to develop, but only one thoughtless moment to destroy, so never use personal information against your friend or reveal any personal information or opinion given to you in confidence.

RESPECT = ACCEPTANCE + EQUALITY

"**M**y best friend listens, does not criticize, and accepts me for who I am."

One friend may be a quiet and shy daydreamer while another is an outgoing and successful professional. A true friend takes you seriously by accepting you with your good points as well as imperfections. People feel respected by their friends when their better characteristics are praised and lesser attributes ignored. By the same token, since most people resent pressure to change, an overcritical friend can lead friendship to disaster. To show you respect your friend you can say,

"I respect your persistence (patience, ability to get along with others, make difficult decisions, etc.)."

"I gained a lot of respect for you when you stood up for yourself in front of our boss (decided to do what was right even though everyone else copped out, admitted you were wrong, gave your opinion even when you were in the minority, etc.)."

"I respect you because you take the risk to follow your dreams (attempt things you've never done before, stand up for what you believe in, care about others, etc.)."

Disagreement among friends is not disrespectful and, in many cases, leads to insightful and stimulating conversation—as long as it does not escalate into a debate with a winner and a loser. If you and your friend do not see eye-to-eye, you can say,

"Let's agree to disagree."

"We obviously see the situation differently, but I respect your point of view."

"We have different points of view, but I respect your opinion."

"I don't agree, but I respect your right to think what you want."

EXCHANGE = NEED + FULFILLMENT

Your contribution to a friendship will dictate what you receive in return. How much effort you invest is important to consider because a vibrant friendship is based on a give-and-take relationship. What you offer your friends is up to you. How much are you willing to become involved in your friend's life? How willing are you to open up and let the other person into your life? Keep in mind that most friendships do not just happen. The reason you become friends with someone is because you both have something to offer and something to gain.

Can you whip up a gourmet meal in no time, while your friend is a klutz in the kitchen? Can your friend drive a golf ball a country mile, while you want to learn the sport? Since most friendships are based on fulfilling needs, sharing skills with friends can add a new dimension to the relationship. For example, if you are shy and your friend is talkative, then he may help you mix more easily at a party. In return, if you are a bargain hunter, you may show him how to outfit a wardrobe without spending a bundle. When friends exchange what they know, they will enchance their friendship. You can say,

"I'd be happy to lend you a hand whenever you need it."

"When you get some free time I'd be happy to show you how to drive a car (play backgammon, go computer shopping, etc.)."

"If I can help you in any way, just let me know."

EMOTIONAL SUPPORT = LAUGHING + CRYING

You don't have to be a perfect friend to be supportive. Are you a warm and affectionate friend? Do you consider yourself sincere, generous, and loyal? Are you willing to do just about anything for a friend? Are you an understanding, sympathetic, and nonjudgmental listener? Are you willing to talk about personal feelings and accept what your friend says without criticism?

Good friendships function on an emotional level with feelings that everyone shares, such as love, hate, sadness, joy, fear, enthusiasm, and so on. Sharing these emotions allows both of you to discuss intimate topics without worrying if you agree on every detail. The important thing is that both of you can open up and share what is on your minds and in your hearts. Sometimes friends will share happy feelings and other times they will share concerns, fears, and self-doubt. As a friend, showing your emotional support plays a vital role in the maintenance of your friendship. You can say,

"I want you to know that I'm your biggest fan."

"I'm behind you all the way."

"I know things are pretty tough for you, but you can count on me."

"If you want to talk about it, I'm always willing to listen."

Asking for emotional support isn't always easy, but it is an important part of friendship. When you want to ask for what you need, then be up-front, yet not too demanding. For example, you can say,

"I'm having a real problem. Do you have a few minutes when we can talk?"

"I trust your judgment. Can I ask you for some advice about something personal?"

"I know this may sound funny, but your support is very important to me."

RECHARGE YOUR FRIENDSHIP BY SHARING NEW ACTIVITIES

Even the best friendship may need recharging once in a while. Rejuvenating a stagnant friendship requires extra effort and imagination by both people. Breathing new life into your friendship is as easy as discussing topics that were touched upon briefly in the past. You can also recharge a friendship by starting a new activity together. For example, you might consider signing up with a friend for a foreign-language course, joining an athletic club, attending a career seminar or a photography or cooking class. To see if your friend is interested, you can say,

"Why don't we get involved in some new activities together? What do you think?"

"I am thinking about taking a microwave cooking class. I think it will be a lot of fun. Do you want to come along?"

"I just found my old tennis racket in the garage and I've decided to take some lessons this summer. Do you still have that old tennis racket of yours? Do you want to join me?"

"You said you always wanted to learn how to speak Spanish and so do I. What do you think about taking a class together?"

As you and your friend learn together, many of the qualities that attracted you to each other in the first place will be highlighted and brought to light through your conversations. So even though you may know each other well, a new learning situation provides an excellent opportunity for both of you to extend your friendship and get to know each other even better. Any activity that allows the two of you to spend more time together will deepen your friendship, partially by allowing you more opportunities for new and intimate conversations.

REESTABLISHING AN OLD FRIENDSHIP IS AS EASY AS A TELEPHONE CALL

"*Hi Jan! This is Lee Jones. I was just thinking of you so I decided to give you a call. What have you been up to for the last three years? I'm coming to town next month and I thought it might be fun to get together to catch up on old times!*"

With today's fast lifestyles and people moving from job to job and place to place, it is no surprise that many good friends lose contact with each other, not because of any disagreement, but simply because their lives have become too busy. Resuming a long-lost friendship is as easy as making a phone call, sending a letter or postcard, or even meeting a friend for a short visit. It is not unusual for friends who shared many interests in the past to quickly pick up where they left off, and even see each other again on a regular basis. Talking about old times and catching up on "what's new" serve as excellent ways to restart the friendship. If you follow up in conversations by sharing new experiences, then you can often resume a full-time friendship.

MAINTAINING LONG-DISTANCE FRIENDSHIPS

People often complain that their friends live far away and that they seldom have the opportunity to talk or see one another. The result? Good friends can allow their valuable relationship to fade away. This unnecessary loss can be avoided with relatively little effort. Consistently showing your friends that you care and think about them will allow both of you to reap some of the many rewards of a close friendship. Even if you live far apart or if you lead different lives than when you first met, the consistent contact will generate the personal interest and warmth needed to keep the friendship growing. Here is the way one person keeps her long-distance friendships growing.

"I exchange postcards, short letters, and phone calls with my friends who live far away. We don't see each other very often, but staying in contact keeps our friendship alive and lets each of us know that we are not lost and gone forever. Now we are planning to get together at our upcoming high school reunion and I can't wait to see them!"

FRIENDSHIP IN THE WORKPLACE

Dear Gabby:

I know several people at work, but I'm not good friends with anyone in particular. One person I know seems open to becoming friends, but I'm not sure how I can turn this acquaintance into a real friendship. Can you help me?

Signed,
Shy

Making a friend at work is easy if you seek a person who shares similar interests and is willing to spend some of his or her free time with you. To turn an acquaintance into a friend follow these four easy steps:

1. SHOW THAT YOU ARE OPEN FOR FRIENDSHIP.

Take the initiative and start a conversation so the other person knows you are interested in becoming friends. Send out friendly signals such as smiling, open body language, chatting casually, suggesting sitting together on coffee breaks, spending time together at lunch, or volunteering to work together on a project. You can say,

"How was your vacation? Are you glad to be back?"

"How did your project finally turn out?"

"I'm looking for a partner on a new project here at work. Are you interested?"

"Do you want to join me for a cup of coffee?"

"Do you have plans for lunch? I know a great place down the street if you'd like to join me."

2. DISCOVER AND TALK ABOUT AT LEAST ONE COMMON INTEREST OUTSIDE OF WORK.

Whether you are making a friend at work or anywhere else, during the time you spend together, seek any common interests upon which you can build an ongoing friendship. To find out a person's interests, listen for "free information" which may give you a hint as to how the other person spends his spare time. For example, if you discover that the other person went hiking over the weekend, you can say,

"Oh you like to go hiking too! So do I! Where did you go? What was it like? What did you enjoy most about your trip?"

"I see that you are reading Backpacker's Catalog. *I've always been interested in hiking, mountain climbing, and just being in the great outdoors. How did you get interested in hiking?"*

"Is backpacking something that you do just for fun or do you want to be a park ranger or something like that?"

3. MAKE PLANS TO SHARE FREE TIME TOGETHER.

To begin your friendship, make an informal date to spend time together after work or on the weekend. Suggest having dinner together, going out for a movie, visiting a museum, attending an adult-education class, going bowling, or any other activity you can enjoy together while you get to know each other better. You can say,

"I read a great review of that play we were talking about yesterday. Would you like to see it with me this weekend?"

"What are you up to this weekend? Are you interested in joining me for a bike ride (fishing expedition, roller-skating, playing softball, going sailing, seeing a concert, etc.)?"

4. TELL YOUR NEW FRIEND THAT YOU HAD A GOOD TIME SHARING A PARTICULAR ACTIVITY AND WANT TO GET TOGETHER AGAIN SOON.

Telling your new friend that you enjoyed spending time together reinforces your desire to get to know each other better and eases the transition from acquaintanceship to friendship. You can say,

"I really enjoyed our bike-riding expedition last weekend! Let's go again soon!"

A note of caution: *"Before you make a friend eat a bushel of salt with him."*

Even though you may be ready to open up and share your private feelings with a prospective friend with whom you work, avoid revealing overly personal information too soon, appearing desperate for company, or seeking someone to solve your problems. You will get to get to know each other naturally by self-disclosing your background, opinions, and feelings at about the same rate and discussing common interest topics. The object is for both of you to think, "I want to get to know this person better."

Generally speaking, becoming a good friend with a coworker can enhance your working relationship if you leave the discussion of personal problems or intimate subject matter for nonworking times. Burdening a coworker/friend with an untimely demand for support or attention while on the job can put a lot of pressure on the friendship. If your friend tries to monopolize your time while you are at work, then try saying,

"I don't mean to cut you short, but I'm terribly busy just now. Besides, I'd rather not talk about anything too personal here because I don't have much privacy. Let's meet after work and have a bite to eat or cup of coffee and then we can talk without being interrupted."

Dear Gabby:

My best friend asked me to get her a job where I work, but I don't think it is a good idea because she is very competitive and I'm not. I'm afraid that working together will put a lot of pressure on our friendship. How can I gracefully decline her request?

Signed,
Noncompetitive Friend

Unhealthy competition in pursuit of career goals can destroy a working relationship and ruin even the best friendships. If you feel that working with your friend may put your friendship in jeopardy, then be up-front about it. You can tactfully decline her request by saying something like,

"You may think that working together would be fun, but there is a lot of pressure and tension between staff members. You're my best friend and I don't want anything to change that, especially some on-the-job problem."

"I think it's best if we don't work together because if something goes wrong on the job and one person feels responsible or gets the blame, then our friendship could really suffer, and I don't want that to happen."

Dear Gabby:

My co-worker (and best friend) just got fired. Is there anything I can say or do to make him feel better?

Signed,
Friend

Invite your friend out to lunch or for a cup of coffee to talk about his dismissal, other potential job opportunities, or unfulfilled career goals he may now pursue. If you do discuss the reasons why your friend was let go, let him do most of the talking by asking questions such as, *"What are your plans?"* or *"How are you feeling about your new situation?"* In this way he can assess the situation without you sounding critical or getting too involved. If you feel comfortable making the offer, say you will be happy to provide your friend with a personal reference. To present an optimistic view of the future, you can be philosophical by saying,

"Sometimes being let go from a job is a blessing in disguise because it forces you to take new risks that you otherwise might pass up. Besides, you never know what new opportunities might come your way!"

TRUE FRIENDSHIP TAKES TIME TO GROW

"**F**riendship: The older it grows, the stronger it gets."

—Proverb

True friendships rarely develop quickly, but rather take considerable time to grow and a willingness of both people to reveal personal feelings. As trust and confidence continue to expand between friends, the other elements that make up a close friendship will fall into place, such as sharing honest feedback, discussing personal problems, and providing confidential advice.

Your best friend knows things about you that no one else may be aware of, including embarrassing secrets, private conversations, and in particular, weaknesses and vulnerabilities. This personal history is the fabric that binds two people together into a true friendship in which loyalty and support are freely given and unquestioned. Best friends confide and help each other accomplish goals, overcome obstacles, and get a perspective on personal problems. They know that the bonds of their relationship are tested and proven in good and bad times alike. After all, isn't that what true friendship is all about?

GABBY GABOR'S
CONVERSATION CLINIC #1
DEALING WITH A JEALOUS OR COMPETITIVE FRIEND

Whether at work or play, a jealous or overcompetitive friend can wreak havoc on your friendship. If you choose to ignore the problem, it will probably get worse. However, if you make a gentle effort to relieve your friend's self-doubts, then your friendship stands a good chance of surviving this all-too-common ailment. The key is to reject the challenge by "stroking" your friend, show your sense of humor, and send the message : "I like you just the way you are."

If your jealous friend says:

"You have all the luck!"

"I wish I was as beautiful (intelligent, rich) as you."

Then you can say:

"You haven't done too badly either."

"You've got a lot going for you!"

"You're not really going to go out with that bum, are you?"

"Maybe. But if you want to call him, be my guest!"

"I'm sure you've got a date this weekend."

"Not really. Anyway I'd rather spend it with you."

If your competitive friend says:

Then you can say:

"I'm finally making more money than you!"

"If it is that important to you, then congratulations! By the way, can I borrow a few bucks?"

"I bet you that I'll make more sales than you this month!"

"I hope you do because then our boss will give both of us a raise!"

"I think we should apply for the same job to see who's best."

"Why worry so much about who's best? We're both good at what we do."

"Let's both date the same person and see who wins out."

"Are you kidding? And lose you as a friend? No way!!"

STOPPING PET PEEVES BEFORE THEY SPOIL YOUR FRIENDSHIP

"**M**y best friend and I used to spend nearly all of our free time together, but now we barely see each other. When we do get together we just argue about stupid things. I really wonder if we are even friends anymore. We both seem to have changed so much since we first met."

LITTLE IRRITATIONS ADD UP TO BIG TROUBLE FOR A FRIENDSHIP

Pet peeves are insidious irritations that creep up on and eat away at the foundation of a friendship. However, if you are assertive and carefully confront your friend's annoying habits you can save your friendship from a slow death.

SYMPTOMS OF A FRIENDSHIP HEADING FOR TROUBLE

From	To
cooperative	argumentative
dependable	irresponsible
open	secretive
patient	intolerant
appreciative	overdemanding
supportive	critical
fun	boring
caring	indifferent
sharing time	being too busy to get together

PET PEEVE #1: A FRIEND WHO CRITICIZES

"*It seems like no matter what I say or do, my friend always criticizes me.*"

How do you feel when a friend responds to your exciting news with critical comments such as, *"What's so good about that?" "Why don't you just give up?"* or *"You should be able to do better than that."* Most people interpret these insensitive comments as demeaning personal attacks, which, if left unchecked, can sap your self-esteem, confidence, and enthusiasm. Even though belittling putdowns can indicate jealousy, envy, unhealthy competition, or low self-esteem on the part of the criticizer, this damaging attitude is a pet peeve that hurts feelings and may ultimately tear your friendship apart.

SOUR GRAPES CAN PERMANENTLY STAIN A FRIENDSHIP

It is natural to feel a little jealous of a friend's success, especially if the two of you are striving for similar personal and professional goals. However, criticizing your friend with snide remarks or failing to acknowledge her accomplishments will surely make your friendship suffer.

Another common complaint is that some friends would rather gripe about mutual problems than talk about more positive subjects. For these friends, if they cannot bellyache and whine about what is going wrong in their lives, then there is little else for them to talk about.

BREAK THE CRITICIZING HABIT

Do you find yourself criticizing your friend instead of lending him or her your support? Putting down a friend with constant criticism can become a habit that will hurt your friendship. Replace criticism with praise and encouragement.

Instead of saying . . .	Say . . .
"I bet this guy is worse than your last boyfriend."	*"What is he like? How did you meet? I hope it works out for you."*
"Have you been putting on weight?"	*"You're looking good!"*
"Your new job sounds like it's a real drag."	*"Every job has its downside. What's the upside?"*
"You call this a great place to live? You've got to be joking! What a dump!"	*"Your new apartment has real potential. What are you going to do first?"*

When you replace criticism with praise you send a message of confidence, enthusiasm, and respect. Your friend will appreciate your comments because they will increase his self-esteem. In addition, praise makes friends more receptive to any suggestions or feedback you may offer.

If you have a friend who just can't pass up an opportunity to put you down or make a critical comment about what you do or hope to accomplish, then try this assertiveness technique to deflect criticism: Simply acknowledge your friend's viewpoint, but rather than let it guide your actions or incite you to a negative retort, proceed as if he or she had been supportive. In other words, accept criticism as a possibility, but don't let it stand in your way or prevent you from reaching your goals.

If Your Friend Says . . .	Then You Can Say . . .
"You aren't going to get the job, so why bother to apply?"	*"You may be right, but I'm going to try anyway and see what happens. I've got nothing to lose."*
"This looks like a lousy place to work."	*"True, it may not be fancy, but I'll see how the job works out before I make any judgments about it."*
"You could never do that in a million years!"	*"Perhaps not, but I'm willing to take a chance."*
"You'll never win, so why put out all that effort?"	*"You're probably right, but at least I'll have given it my best shot."*

Dear Gabby:

Is there a way to give a friend constructive feedback without starting a fight or sounding overcritical?

Signed,
Honest Friend

Feedback is a valuable tool that allows you to show genuine interest in your friend's goals as you offer insights, suggestions, and support. And, if feedback is presented properly, it encourages your friend to ask for your opinions in the future. However, your friend must be receptive to your comments if they are to be helpful and not hurtful. To determine if your friend even wants your feedback, you can ask,

"Are you interested in a second opinion?"

"Do you want me to give you any feedback?"

"Do you want to know what I think about it?"

Note: If your friend chooses not to seek your feedback or declines your offer, accept that decision and keep your opinions to yourself.

CAUTION: EVEN WELL - INTENDED CRITICISM CAN BACKFIRE

Many people may not realize that even well-intended criticism can make a friend feel inferior, depressed, or let down. Instead of helping, criticism can leave your friend emotionally deflated and resentful at your bringing up the subject in the first place, depending on the manner in which you give your criticism and how receptive your friend is.

The best kind of feedback is that which allows your friend to accept or reject your opinions or suggestions, without making you feel slighted. When you offer feedback in a "for what it's worth" format, if it helps, great! If not, well that's okay too. The following tips will help you present nonthreatening feedback.

- Be sensitive to your friend's feelings. Offer your comments as suggestions and opinions, not as ultimatums and definitive statements.

- Restate what your friend has said to show that you have listened carefully and understand his or her viewpoint or conclusion.

- To establish receptivity for your comments and suggestions, highlight and praise as many positive aspects of your friend's endeavor as possible. You can say, *"I really like the way you . . ."* *"That part of the . . . works well."* *"I think you are right on target when you say . . ."*

- Ask for clarification of what you do not understand or agree with by saying, *"There is one thing I don't understand. How does . . . fit in?"*

- See how your friend responds to your first comments before offering additional feedback. If he is defensive, then pull back and let him talk. If he seems open to your suggestions, then continue. You can also ask how he feels about your feedback by asking, *"What do you think about my comments?"* *"Are they helpful?"* *"Am I on target with your way of thinking?"* *"Do you want me to continue?"*

- When offering suggestions, avoid using words like, *"You should do . . ."* *"Why don't you . . . ?"* *"Don't you think that . . . ?"* Instead, you can say, *"Perhaps you might consider . . ."* *"Here is an idea that might work . . ."* *"What do you think of this approach?"*

- If you disagree with your friend, you can say directly, *"I'm not crazy about that idea. That approach doesn't do much for me. I'd like to see something different."*

- Always respect your friend's right to accept or reject your feedback by saying, *"Here is what I think—feel free to take it or leave it."*

PET PEEVE #2: A FRIEND WHO CONSTANTLY COMPLAINS

"If I hear one more complaint about his bossy supervisor, lousy love life, or boring graduate course, I think I'm going to hang up our friendship!"

Does your friend expect you to listen quietly as he unloads an endless stream of problems and worries? Constant complaining about an unfulfilling job, poor health, unsatisfying love relationships, lack of money, or other troubles can make you feel used and bored! While being a good listener is one of the great expectations of friendship, some people abuse a friend's willingness to listen by overwhelming him with complaints about personal problems. If a "poor little old me" conversation continues too long, an understanding friend will become disinterested and unsympathetic because most people have little patience for someone who does nothing to make changes or find solutions to personal problems. It is for this reason that persistent complaining is yet another pet peeve that can bring down even the best friendship.

Dear Gabby:

Whenever I get a phone call from my old college buddy, she always monopolizes the conversation with all of her trials and tribulations. She rarely asks how I'm feeling or what's new in my life, and if she does ask, the subject quickly changes back to her. I've reached the point where I avoid picking up the phone from fear of being trapped in a two-hour, one-way conversation of nonstop complaints. I still like my friend, but she is driving me crazy! What can I do?

Signed,
Tired of Listening

TO STOP THE COMPLAINER, CHANGE THE SUBJECT

The next time you find yourself trapped on the telephone with a complainer, try the following techniques to break the pattern and change the subject to a more balanced and upbeat conversation:

1. Say that you have a limited time to talk (five to fifteen minutes). For example, *"Hi Sam, how are you? Your boss is on your case again? That's too bad. I'm fine, but I'm on my way to an appointment (expecting a phone call, going to the store, sitting down to a meal, etc.), so I only have a few minutes to chat."*
Note: While an excuse may be less than the complete truth, the idea is to let your friend know that your time is valuable and that you have better things to do than to sit and listen to endless complaining.

2. After listening for a few moments, send the message to your friend that you would rather talk about something else. Redirect the conversation away from the friend's problems by summing up her situation, and then asking a question or volunteering some information of your own about a topic you wish to discuss. You can say, *"Gee it sounds like your job is driving you nuts. But let me change the topic for a moment. I've decided to take a vacation next month and wanted to ask you for the name of that travel agent you mentioned the last time we talked."*

To take the conversational ball away from your friend you may have to interrupt her several times over a period of a minute or two. This will slow down your friend's incessant complaining and establish you as the new speaker with a new topic.

3. If your friend turns the conversation back to her problems, you may want to make an action-oriented statement such as, *"Maybe it is time for some action. How about taking some risks? What are your options?"* Encouraging discussion about short-term and long-term changes will turn the conversation away from passive complaining to active problem-solving. However, do not be surprised if your friend continues to wallow in her misfortune. If you are lucky, once your friend comes up with a few options she can act upon, you can change the subject to one in which you are more interested.

4. If your friend still does not get the message that you do not want to hear her sob stories, say in a friendly, but firm voice, *"I'm sorry to hear that you're so unhappy. Maybe it would help if we talk about something else."*

5. To end the conversation you can say, *"I've got to go now, but I hope you are feeling better soon."* Then close the conversation with a friendly good-bye. This direct yet supportive message says, *"I still like you, but I don't want to continually talk about your problems."*

A PESSIMISTIC OUTLOOK CAN KILL YOUR FRIENDSHIP

Why does it matter if you present a pessimistic outlook to a friend? Most people like friends who can focus on the brighter side of life and make others feel good about themselves. A person who constantly complains is looked upon as a pessimist and rarely makes others feel comfortable. As a result, a friend may feel that it will not be long before he too comes under the over-critical eye of the pessimist. When this happens, the friendship can become so uncomfortable that it may collapse.

PET PEEVE #3: A FRIEND WHO ASKS FOR TOO MANY FAVORS

"**I** *just can't say no to a friend.*"

Some friends are too nice for their own good. Does your friend take advantage of your kind nature by asking you for numerous favors? While most people are happy to help out a buddy once in a while, trouble can develop if an overdemanding friend asks too many favors or makes inconsiderate requests. This pet peeve is one of the most aggravating and problematic ones, because a giving friend can quickly feel used and unappreciated. Asking a friend for occasional favors is fine unless they add up to *"What do you want out of me now?"* If a friend feels this way, making too many requests can put a warm friendship permanently on ice.

IF YOU DO NOT WANT TO GRANT A FAVOR, THEN SAY NO

While it is difficult for some people to deny a request from a friend, sometimes it is necessary. Take the attitude that you have the right to say no and do not have to defend your decision too vigorously. However, you can reinforce your position by saying, *"I understand that you want me to . . ."* Then restate the request and firmly say, *"I have my reasons for saying no and they are . . ."* Give the most important reason first, keep your explanations brief, and stick to the point. Then finish with, *"The answer is no."*

Here are some other tactful ways to deny a friend a favor:

"Sorry, now is not a good time for me."

"Gee, I'd really like to help you out, but I'm so busy right now I don't know which end is up."

"I would if I could, but I can't."

"Under normal circumstances I'd be happy to help, but you've caught me at a bad time."

HOW TO ASK A FRIEND FOR A FAVOR

Dear Gabby:

I need to ask a friend for a special favor, but I'm afraid that I may be asking too much of him because he has done so many favors for me in the past. How can I

*ask for another favor without making him feel that I
am just taking advantage of his good nature or our
friendship?*

Signed,
Friend in Need

The best policy when asking a friend a favor is to be
up-front, while at the same time giving him an out if he
is unable or unwilling to grant your request. If your
friend has done a lot of favors for you, showing your
appreciation before asking for another favor is important, or your friend may feel like you are trying to manipulate him into doing something else for you. To avoid
this dilemma in the first place, do not ask for unnecessary favors. Then when you really need a special favor
from a friend, you will not feel like you are asking too
much of your friendship. How do you know when or
when not to ask a favor?

1. First ask yourself,

- Is this favor reasonable? If not, don't ask.

- Can you do it yourself, or are you relying on your
  friend to make your life easier at his expense? If
  yes, then don't ask.

- Can your friend fulfill your request without undue
  inconvenience or hardship? If not, don't ask.

2. If you truly need a favor from a friend, then be
straightforward with your request. Never attempt to
manipulate your friend through guilt or insincere
warmth. To be direct you can say something like,

"I want to ask you for a favor."

"Can you help me out with a small favor?"

"I was wondering if you can lend me a hand with . . . ?"

"If it is not too much trouble, would you be willing to do me a favor?"

3. Always allow your friend the option to decline your request. You can say,

"If you would rather not, just say so. I'll understand."

"If it is inconvenient, no problem. I'll work something else out."

"Please feel free to say no."

4. Be sure to tell your friend how much you appreciate him doing you the favor. That way your friend won't feel like you are taking him for granted. You can say,

"Thanks for the favor. I really appreciate it. If there is anything I can do for you, please just let me know."

"I just want to tell you how much I appreciate what you've done for me lately. You're a good friend."

"Thanks for all the help you've given me. You're a real pal."

PET PEEVE #4: A FRIEND WHO IS ALWAYS LATE

Dear Gabby:

I have a friend who can't get anywhere on time—ever! Being forty-five minutes late for a lunch date is typical, but when she showed up two hours late for Thanksgiving dinner because she couldn't decide on what to wear I hit the roof. Her habitual lateness is seriously undermining our friendship. Is there anything I can do?

Signed,
Angry Friend

Being late is one of the most annoying pet peeves a person can inflict on a friendship. For some people, getting to a specific place on time seems just about impossible. Usually the chronically late person does not realize—or fails to acknowledge—how inconsiderate it is to keep a friend waiting. When your friend consistently prances in late with a lame comment such as *"Better late than never!"* this does little more than imply that you have nothing better to do with your time than to wait around for your tardy pal. After a while you may reach the point of not wanting to see your friend at all, and *boom*—there goes the friendship down the drain.

To stop this pet peeve before it is too late, take an assertive stand when you make your next date to meet and use the following six-point strategy:

1. Call the night before to confirm your date. Point out that you are busy tomorrow, but still want to get together. You can say, *"Hi Jill, I'm just calling to make* *sure we are still on for lunch tomorrow. I've got a busy day at work, but I'm looking forward to seeing you, so please be on time."*

2. Pick a convenient place to meet that provides you with some distraction while you wait—such as a bookstore, park bench, or gift shop.

3. Repeat when and where you expect to meet. If your friend is hopeless when it comes to being on time, suggest a half hour before you really want to meet. You can say, *"We are meeting tomorrow between eleven-thirty A.M. and noon inside the Quiet Bookstore. It is on the corner of Main Street and First Avenue."*

4. Emphasize that you want her to be punctual because you have a limited amount of time to spend together. You can say, *"I would appreciate it if you are there no later than noon because I have to get back to work by one P.M."*

5. Ask her to repeat the specific time and place you plan to meet. You can say, *"I just want to make sure that we have the same information for tomorrow. Tell me, when and where are we meeting?"*

6. Finally, ask your friend to give you a call if she is going to be more than fifteen minutes late. You can say, *"Jill, please do me a favor and call me if you are running behind schedule. I won't have time to wait around for you if you are late."*

If your friend makes a habit of arriving late, you may want to point out that waiting for her is annoying at best, and at worse, makes you feel like she is taking your availability for granted. While these might sound like strong words, being up-front and assertive is the best way to correct your friend's tardiness. If you do not tell your friend that her lateness bothers you, then do not expect her to change and be on time.

BEING ASSERTIVE IS THE MOST EFFECTIVE WAY TO STOP PET PEEVES FROM SPOILING YOUR FRIENDSHIP

If your friend is overcritical, complains endlessly, is too demanding, or always late, then your friendship may be suffering. However, if you take the risk to assertively discuss these or other pet peeves before they become major problems, then you can prevent these insidious troublemakers from ruining your friendship.

GABBY GABOR'S
CONVERSATION CLINIC #2
HOW TO SAY NO TO A FRIEND

Sometimes a friend will ask you for a favor. If it is convenient, then do what you can, because that is part of friendship. However, there are situations when you do not have the time or the inclination, or when the request is inappropriate. An assertive way to deny a friend's request is to repeat "No" as many times as is necessary. This "broken record" technique works well for persistent friends! Be direct, firm, and friendly, and do not feel guilty. If you do not want to do a friend a favor, say, "No, I don't want to do that!"

The Favor (To Lend Your Car):
"Can I borrow your car to go down to the liquor store to get another six-pack?"

The Answer:
"No. It's against the law to drink and drive, plus I am the only person insured to drive my car. Sorry, the answer is no."

The Favor (To Lend Money):
"Will you loan me a hundred dollars? I promise I'll pay you back just as soon as I get home from the track."

The Answer:
"I'm short right now. Sorry I can't help you out."

The Favor (To Tell a "Little White Lie"):
"Can't you just say that I was at the meeting? No one will ever know—just you and me."

The Answer:
"No. That's one you'll have to handle on your own. I'd rather not get involved."

The Favor (The "Little Fix-It Favor"):
"Can you help me fix the sink? I'm sure you can fix it in no time."

The Answer:
"I'm sorry but I'm busy at the moment so I can't help you. Anyhow, I think this is a job for a professional."

The Favor (An Illegal Investment):
"Hey buddy! I've got a 'sure deal' that will make us rich—overnight. All we need is some cash. Are you interested?"

The Answer:
"No thanks. I think I'll pass on that idea."

PREDICTABLE CHANGES THAT ROCK FRIENDSHIPS

Most friendships go through predictable ups and downs due to lifestyle changes such as finding a new job, a new friend, or a new love relationship, getting married, having children, or getting divorced. The keys to preserving an established friendship are the ability to anticipate a friend's changes and the flexibility to adjust to them accordingly.

As people change, so do their friendships. Sometimes the people grow in similar ways, and other times they do not. If you anticipate a certain amount of ebb and flow in your friendship, then adjusting to the changes will be easier than if your expectations are rigid or you overlook predictable events. It is especially helpful to talk to your friend about the changes you see taking place so you can reaffirm your friendship. Even if your friendship drifts apart for a while it can eventually grow back together again if you allow each other room to grow independently.

PREDICTABLE CHANGE #1: ONE FRIEND STARTS A NEW JOB

"**P**hil *completely changed after starting his new job. I never thought my old hang-loose buddy would become so uptight. We almost never see each other and I feel like we don't have much in common anymore.*"

A new job means new responsibilities, an expanded social calendar, new business contacts, and new friends. All of these can cut into an existing friendship, leaving an old buddy feeling left in the dust. In addition, a friend's new job may represent a change in goals, which can also cause conflict in the friendship. For example, if two carefree pals spend most of their time together, and then one friend decides to get a steady job, the friendship may suffer.

A NEW JOB MEANS LESS TIME FOR AN OLD FRIEND

When you make a major career change, your friendships will change too. In most cases, there will be less time devoted to old friends and more time given to the new job. The best way to lessen the impact of a job change is to talk about it openly. If you are the one making the change you might say,

"I've been ready for a challenging new job for a long time and I've finally found one! The problem is that I won't be around as much anymore, but we can still get together on the weekends."

"I'm sorry to say that my extended vacation is over because I've just got a new job that will take up nearly all my time. We'll still get to spend some time together, but just not as much as we used to."

WHAT IF YOU ARE THE ONE WHO FEELS ABANDONED?

Feeling abandoned is natural when a friend makes a change that does not include you. When you spend a lot of time with someone and then suddenly you are on your own, it can be upsetting and lonely. Rather than making your friend feel guilty, however, keep in mind that your friend's career change is a personal decision, and that an overcritical or jealous attitude on your part will lead your friendship into trouble. Even if you do not like the fact that your friend is making a change, be supportive by saying,

"I'd like to hear about your new job."

"Your new job sounds like a real challenge. I'm sure that you'll do great! Congratulations and best of luck!"

"What are the people like that you are going to be working with?"

"What do you think you are going to like best about your new job?"

If you are still troubled by your friend's career move, then you might bring up the subject by saying,

"I never realized you were interested in . . . What made you decide to take that kind of job?"

"Gee, I'm going to miss you. I understand that you will be busy, but I hope we can still go fishing (bowling, shopping, etc.) together."

PREDICTABLE CHANGE #2: ONE PERSON MAKES A NEW FRIEND

Dear Gabby:

Ellen and I used to be best friends until Kim came along. Now they are best friends and I'm the odd one out. How can I tell her than I'm hurt and want to see her more without sounding petty and jealous?

Signed,
Hurt Friend

A NEW FRIEND CAN BE A THREAT TO AN OLD FRIEND

While a best friendship can be as exclusive as a love relationship, even the greatest buddy in the world cannot fulfill all the needs of friendship. It is not surprising that when a person makes a new friend, a previously established friendship can get thrown off, much to the old friend's disadvantage. A new friendship brings more activities and obligations, which can leave less time for the old friend. The friend who once had top priority may now feel left out, rejected, or treated like a second fiddle because her best-friend status has been usurped by someone new. If an unhealthy competition develops, it can provoke jealousy, resentment, pettiness, anger, and hurt feelings for everyone involved. If the old friend is alone, her bitterness and sense of loss may be compounded. She may feel betrayed and withdraw completely, leaving your friendship in the dust.

WHAT IF YOU ARE THE FRIEND WHO IS LEFT OUT?

If you are the hurt friend, why not say how you really feel? True, it takes guts to put your feelings on the line, but your friend will value your honesty and, hopefully, be more sensitive to you. You can say something like,

"I'm feeling a little upset because we used to spend a lot more time together and now I hardly even hear from you. Aren't we still friends?"

"I know you've made some new friends at work, and I don't want to sound petty or put pressure on you, but I'd like to spend more time together, like we used to. What do you say?"

SAVING THE OLD FRIENDSHIP

It is perfectly natural for your old buddy to feel jealous if you make a new friend. But does making a new friend mean that you will lose your old friend? Not if you are sensitive to your old friend's feelings and take steps to strengthen your friendship. If you sense that she is anxious about your new acquaintance, reinforce your best friend's role in your life by saying,

"Our friendship goes way back and that is very special to me."

"We've been best friends for a long time and no one is going to change that."

"Old friends, like old wine, are best!"

ALLOW EXTRA TIME FOR AN OLD FRIENDSHIP

Kind words alone, however, are not enough to lessen a friend's fears; they must be backed up by personal contact. If you value your friendship, give it some extra time, even if it means giving up some time with your new friend. This will make your old pal feel that she still has a high priority in your life. If you think your new and old friend will hit it off, make an effort to blend the two relationships. Sometimes an old friend will feel less threatened if she is included in the new friendship too. Above all, keep in mind that true best friends are few and far between because they have passed the test of time and trust. If you consider your friendship special, give it the respect, consideration, and time that it deserves. If you do, you can still make new friends without falling prey to this predictable pitfall. To let your good friend know that you value your friendship you can say,

"I know I've been busy lately, but how about joining me for dinner this weekend? I've missed talking with you."

"I've met a friend I think you would really like. We are going to a movie tonight. Would you like to join us?"

"I heard that our favorite jazz group is playing in town this week and I've finally got a few nights free. Do you want to see their show or maybe just catch up on what's been happening?"

PREDICTABLE CHANGE #3:
ONE FRIEND FALLS IN LOVE

Dear Gabby:

Since my friend fell in love, he never returns my calls and acts like I don't even exist. He is so wrapped up in his new love affair that he acts like he could care less about me or any of his other friends. I understand that being in love is the best thing in the world, but I don't like being treated as if my feelings don't count. Any advice?

Signed,
Jealous Friend

A friendship always changes when one friend falls in love. When two people fall in love they spend more time together and less time with their friends because the excitement of a new love affair is an easy winner over a well-known, and sometimes well-worn, friendship. Since single people often base their friendships on a mutual availability, one person's involvement in a love relationship represents a major change that can make the single friend feel deserted and displaced like a rejected lover.

WHAT IF YOU ARE THE ONE WHO FEELS JEALOUS?

Most old friends cannot compete with a friend's lover, so why bother to try? To do so just makes everyone feel uncomfortable and resentful. It is more productive to accept the changed situation without sounding like a rejected lover crying for attention, but at the same time tell your friend that you would like to see more of him or her. Use a bit of humor and say something like,

"I'm happy that you are so much in love, but let's try to get together before the next ice age sets in."

"I haven't heard from you in so long, I thought maybe you dropped off the face of the earth. Why don't we get together again sometime soon?"

"Since we are having trouble linking up, why not have my answering machine have lunch with your answering machine. That way at least we'll know what each of us is up to."

IT'S UP TO THE FRIEND IN LOVE TO MAKE TIME FOR THE OLD FRIEND

Even if you are not spending as much time with your friend as you once were, showing that you still want to keep the friendship active will reinforce your feelings for each other. If you tell your friend that you value his friendship it will help minimize the hard feelings that often crop up between best friends and a new lover. To reassure your old friend and avoid this pitfall, you can say,

"Being in love is great, but nobody can replace a best friend like you. How about getting together for lunch or dinner sometime soon?"

"I know I've been hard to reach lately, but I want to get together with you soon. When are you free?"

"Don't be shy about giving me a call. I miss talking with you on the phone and so much has happened since we last spoke. I want to tell you everything!"

Someday you will probably want to introduce your friend to your new lover. In many cases, if a noncompetitive atmosphere is established early on, then the love relationship can continue to flourish without sacrificing the best friendship. However, it is vital for the single friend to recognize that the desire in most people for a secure love relationship is so strong, that in the end, if the friend does not compromise, the friendship may be lost. But if the situation presents itself, the single friend may find that her friend's lover can become a good friend too.

PREDICTABLE CHANGE #4:
ONE FRIEND GETS MARRIED

Marriage usually causes predictable changes in friendship, and even though it is a happy time for the marrying friend, the single friend may resent the shift in allegiance. You can help alleviate your friend's doubts about your loyalty by saying,

"Even though I am getting married, you're still my best friend."

"I'm looking forward to getting settled so you and I can get together on a more regular basis again."

A NEW SET OF RULES FOR SINGLE FRIENDS

Single friends have their own set of rules. For example, it may be fine to call or visit any time of day or night, walk into the other's home unannounced, or fix a snack without asking permission or cleaning up afterward. However, when one friend marries, all that changes. The married friend may be available only at certain times, midnight telephone calls are disturbing, spontaneous jaunts to the twenty-four-hour doughnut shop are a thing of the past, and leaving a mess behind is absolutely out of the question. Marriage brings a new set of rules to an old friendship, so if the old best friend wants to remain welcome, then he or she must be flexible and follow the new ways of doing things. To ease the transition between you and a newly married friend you can say,

"Now that you are married I know your schedule is going to change, so tell me, how late can I call without causing a problem?"

"Please let me know if I need to adjust any of my habits around your house. I don't want to cause any friction with your new spouse."

KEEP YOUR SINGLE FRIENDS EVEN AFTER YOU MARRY

If you marry, you will probably form new friendships with other couples, and though this can cause conflict with some of your single friends, there is no reason to end an old friendship. Sharing time with your best friend and spouse is a good way to break down the natural barriers between them while at the same time allowing two important people in your life the opportunity to get to know each other better. To make your single friend feel welcome in your new arrangement you can say,

"Would you like to come over and join us tonight for dinner (a movie, cards, ball game, walk in the park, etc.)? Ellen would like to get to know you better."

PREDICTABLE CHANGE #5:
ONE FRIEND BECOMES A PARENT

"**A**fter my friend had her first child our friendship nearly went down the tubes."

Finally, nothing can change a friend like parenthood. A single friend with plenty of time on her hands is a faint memory after she marries and has a child. There are diapers to change, day-care to arrange, parent meetings to attend, and a lifetime of other "must do" items. The most frequent loser in this situation is the new parent's best friend. Why? It is difficult at best to have enough time for a spouse, a job, home, shopping, and the myriad other responsibilities that go along with raising a family. There's not much time left to maintain a full-time friendship too. Nevertheless, you can still be a good friend by showing interest in the new child. You can say,

"How do you like being a new parent?" "What's the latest with your baby?" "I want you to know I really envy you. I think your baby is beautiful!"

But becoming a parent almost always means making new friends, too. Other parents with children replace single friends as confidants because the new parent seeks people with whom he or she can share child-rearing experiences, problems, and strategies, as well as other aspects of friendship. This change from an independent, career-minded, single person to that of a family-oriented spouse and parent places increased pressure on even the best friendships.

A CHILD'S POOR BEHAVIOR CAN SOUR YOUR FRIENDSHIP

"**I** love my friend dearly, but her kid drives me up a wall."

Another troublesome area between best friends is child-rearing. Single friends may have their ideas and expectations of how children should behave and how parents ought to dole out discipline. Parents, of course, have their child-rearing theories too, but practicality, compromise, flexibility, and common sense become more important than theory.

SAY NOTHING CRITICAL ABOUT YOUR FRIEND'S CHILD-REARING PRACTICES

Do not criticize your friend's child-rearing techniques or the child's behavior. Criticism is usually interpreted as disapproval and is probably not appreciated or welcome. Since parents raise their children in the way that they think is best, it is better to keep your criticism to yourself, unless you are asked for your opinion. Then give it gently and with the comment, *"Feel free to ignore my advice."* However, if you are critical, be aware that a parent will defend her child like a cornered mother bear will protect her cubs—to the death! If your friend criticizes you or your child, then you can say,

"I can appreciate you being uncomfortable around a fussy (misbehaving, clinging, etc.) child, but I am doing what I think is best."

"I know you're no expert, but how would you suggest that I handle the problem?"

"I can see that we have different approaches to child-rearing, but I'll think about your suggestion."

IF YOU VALUE YOUR FRIENDSHIP, GET A SITTER!

Not everyone loves children. In fact, there are some adults who feel uncomfortable around children who are simply acting like kids. If your best friend falls into this category, then consider planning some time together without your child. By making arrangements for a sitter, in-law, or another parent to cover for you one afternoon or evening, you and your friend can enjoy each other's company without you having to keep one eye on your child. This demonstrates that your friendship is still an important part of your life. On the other hand, if your parent-friend fails to pick up on your desire to be with her, but without her kids along, you can say,

"How would you feel about us spending some time together without your kids?"

"How about getting a sitter for some afternoon so we can meet for lunch and go shopping like we did in the old days?"

"I like your kids, but it would be fun if just the two of us could go out alone some afternoon."

PREDICTABLE CHANGE #6: DIVORCE

Dear Gabby:

My best friend just got a divorce. What can I say to him that will help him get through this unhappy time?

Signed,
Concerned (and also divorced) Friend

Best friends are famous for saying, *"I could have told you it wasn't going to last."* Judgmental comments like this only make your friend feel worse and do little to help him cope with the situation. Supportive statements say that you have confidence that he will live through the experience, painful though it may be, and that he will be able to carry on with his life. You can say,

"I know how you feel, but the pain will pass."

"You are a survivor and so is she, so don't worry, you'll both get through it."

"It won't be easy, but you are a strong person and you will make it."

"It takes some time to get back on your feet, but you'll be back in action in no time."

"As my mother always said, 'There's plenty of fish in the sea!' "

If either party to a divorce tries to get you to take sides, then you can be a good friend to both people without getting involved in the inevitable blame and anger that accompanies separation or divorce. If either divorcing friend asks you to take sides you can say,

"I'd rather remain neutral since I'm friends with both of you."

"I think it would be best if I don't get directly involved."

GABBY GABOR'S
CONVERSATION CLINIC #3
HOW TO BE A SUPPORTIVE FRIEND

Being an enthusiastic, nonjudgmental friend is one of the most important components of a good friendship. A supportive person does not cast blame, lecture, manipulate, ridicule, or pass judgment on another's deeds, dreams, or feelings, but rather listens quietly, providing honest feedback when asked, and being sympathetic to a friend's difficulties. Being understanding makes the difference between a relationship of convenience and one of true friendship. Even though you cannot solve your friend's problems, you can make his or her trials and tribulations a lot easier to cope with.

Instead of Saying . . .

"*Who cares?*"

"*I told you so!*"

Say . . .

"*I understand how you feel.*"

"*No one can predict the future.*"

"I could have told you it wasn't going to work out."

"No one knows if a marriage is going to be successful. It is always a gamble."

"There is nothing to getting a divorce."

"I know this is a difficult time but you'll survive it."

"You'll never be able to live without each other."

"Don't worry, you can make it on your own."

"You'll never get that new job."

"Go for it! I wish you luck on getting the job."

"Face it! You couldn't do that if you wanted to."

"You have nothing to lose by trying."

"You're too old for that sort of thing."

"It's never too late to learn something new."

"What makes you think you are so special?"

"You've got a lot going for you. Don't cut yourself short!"

FIXING

A

FRACTURED

FRIENDSHIP

It seems inevitable that sooner or later sparks will fly between friends. If you value your friendship, then it is worth resolving a conflict. By exploring each of the following options you can formulate a strategy that can heal a fractured friendship. You may find more than one option will be helpful, but keep in mind that not all issues can be resolved immediately. Nevertheless, if you take the risk to talk about an outstanding issue, your friendship will probably flourish once again.

Dear Gabby:

I have a friend who made me so mad the other night I could scream! We hadn't seen each other in months (she had broken several previous dates to meet) and when we did finally get together, she got so drunk and obnoxious that we got into a fight. We've been good friends for many years, but I felt like I never wanted to see her again. What can I say to make her understand that she really hurt my feelings without making it sound like I'm making a mountain out of a mole hill?

Signed,
Hurt Friend

OPTION #1: BE DIRECT AND TELL YOUR FRIEND WHY YOU ARE ANGRY

Although your reasons for being angry may be perfectly obvious to you, counting on a friend to know why you are upset can be deadly for the friendship. You may hope for changes in your friend's actions, but meanwhile if she is unaware how you feel or what you expect, then you are likely to be disappointed and resentful. Many unassertive people fear expressing their anger even when saying what is on their mind presents the best chance of resolving the problem. To be assertive you can say,

"I value our friendship too much not to say what's on my mind. I am angry and I want you to know why."

"I do not appreciate being canceled out at the last minute just because someone called you with a better offer."

"It makes me feel angry to think that my friendship is taken for granted."

"I feel that I deserve more consideration."

"I just wanted you to know how I felt. As far as I am concerned the matter is closed."

ASSERTIVENESS CAN SAVE A FRIENDSHIP

If you choose to remain unassertive and silent, then resentment will ultimately replace affection in your friendship, leaving it a cold and unemotional relationship. If this cooling trend is not reversed, then your friendship can be permanently damaged. On the other hand, it takes courage to discuss a troubling issue, talking it through to an acceptable conclusion. Confronting a friend is uncomfortable, but it releases anger in a beneficial way and can prevent a small problem from growing out of proportion.

YOUR FRIEND MAY HAVE A GRIPE TOO

If you bring up an issue that is bothering you, do not be surprised if your friend takes the opportunity to do the same thing. If she reveals a sore point concerning your past behavior, you can say,

"I wish you had told me about it before, but now I know. I'm sorry if I caused you a problem. Next time I do something that bothers you, please tell me. We are good enough friends to be honest with each other."

OPTION #2: LIMIT YOUR CONVERSATIONS TO NONPERSONAL TOPICS

Dear Gabby:

My friend has so many personal problems that our conversations always seem to end up in therapy sessions about his troubles. I like my friend, but I feel uncomfortable when he asks me for advice because I don't know what to say or how to help him. How can I change the topic of conversation away from his problems without making him feel like I am being insensitive?

Signed,
Frustrated Friend

An unhappy friend can become troublesome and dependent. He or she often seeks help from others, with the burden of support usually falling onto close family or friends. While assistance freely offered during a temporary crisis is a reasonable expectation, an overly dependent friend can ruin a friendship if he or she expects you to act as a "safety net." If you have a friend whose troubles are overwhelming, then limit the scope of your conversations to exclude discussion of his personal problems. By doing so you encourage a dependent friend to become more independent and find solutions to his problems. When he starts in on the same old pattern of complaining, sympathize by saying that you understand, and then change the topic to more mutually rewarding subjects. For example, you can say,

"I understand how you are feeling, but I'm only your friend— I can't solve your problems. Only you can do that. Why don't

we talk about something else. Have you seen any good movies or read any good books lately?"

"It sounds like you are asking me for advice, but I honestly don't know what to tell you, except that you can make the changes in your life that you want—if you are willing to take some action. Speaking of making changes, I'm going to look at a new apartment. Do you want to come along?"

When you take this assertive stance you are:

- limiting your involvement in your friend's problems.

- encouraging a dependent friend to become more independent.

- maintaining the positive part of your friendship by focusing on the mutually rewarding aspects, not one person's personal problems.

- avoiding a complete breakdown of the friendship.

SUGGESTING PROFESSIONAL HELP FOR A FRIEND

If a friend suffers from chronic problems, including alcohol or drug abuse, then your best intentions will not be enough to solve his troubles. Suggesting that your friend seek a properly trained mental health professional for advice is one way to help a person cope with a crisis situation without becoming directly involved. You can say,

"I'm not a therapist (doctor, money manager, etc.). There are trained people who can help with the sorts of problems you are having. Why not consider getting professional help?"

OPTION #3: PUT THE FRIENDSHIP "ON HOLD"

Dear Gabby:

I've tried everything to get my best friend to talk about our fight, but she is unwilling. What can I do?

Signed,
Giving Up

There may come a time when you are so frustrated with a friendship that you are ready to throw in the towel and give up the whole relationship. Perhaps your friend is pressuring you too much or is being so argumentative that the friendship is not worth the trouble. However, instead of ending the friendship forever, you can put it on hold by withdrawing for a while to allow both of you time to think the situation over. This option allows the door to be left open for reconciling your friendship sometime in the future. While this conversation is not an easy one, it will be less stressful if you plan what you want to say before you say it. One effective way to organize your thoughts is to write them down. Once you know what you want to say, remain calm and controlled. Don't resort to being bitter, sarcastic, or accusatory. Whether you tell your friend how you feel in person, by phone, or in a letter, you can say,

"I am unhappy with the way we are communicating and I think we both need time to think about our friendship."

"I would like to remain friends but I cannot accept our friendship as it is. I've tried to tell you about my feelings, but we just can't seem to communicate like we used to."

"Our conversations need to change before I will feel comfortable about our friendship again, but I want you to know that I am willing to talk about it anytime you are. I wish that I felt differently. Maybe sometime later we can start our friendship again."

OPTION #4: MAKE UP AND BE FRIENDS AGAIN

Good friendships are rare and worth saving—even if they occasionally run into trouble. Sadly, many people let go of their good friendships far too easily. Arguments between friends are common enough, so why avoid confronting an issue that could turn into an oppportunity to revitalize your friendship? In the long run, if you care about each other, you may be able to sort out your differences and resume the friendship. If you approach a separation as a temporary measure, then your friendship will have a good chance of starting up again when both of you are willing to talk about and resolve outstanding issues, or to forgive and forget. Since people and circumstances change, some time apart will enable both of you to get a new appreciation for your friendship. When you feel enough time has passed, suggest that the two of you become friends again and see how he or she responds. In many cases, both people want to make up but are afraid to make the first move. You can say,

"I know we've had some disagreements, but I'd like to be friends again."

"I want you to know that I am not angry anymore. How are you feeling?"

"As far as I'm concerned past is past. I think our friendship is worth much more than who's right or wrong."

A TIME TO FORGET THE PAST AND MOVE THE FRIENDSHIP FORWARD

The saying "Time heals all wounds" applies here. At a certain point past mistakes, indiscretions, and irritations lose their importance and mutual affection returns to a best friendship. The desire to reconcile the friendship outweighs any argument, anger, insensitivity, or jealousy that may have sparked the disagreement in the first place.

GABBY GABOR'S
CONVERSATION CLINIC #4

TELLING A FRIEND WHY YOU ARE ANGRY

Keep in mind that there are risks when confronting a friend with your disapproval or anger, so be sure you are not being oversensitive, defensive, or overreacting to criticism, a joke, or a glib remark. If you have a good reason to be angry, then be assertive by speaking calmly and clearly. Don't beat around the bush—be direct! But keep your sense of humor—you'll need it!

---

1. Plan your comments before approaching your friend so you can specifically describe your feelings. Write them down on a sheet of paper, if necessary.

2. Say, *"Hi . . . Do you have a few minutes? There is something I'd like to talk to you about."*

3. Say, *"I'm feeling angry (disappointed, let down, etc.). I expected more consideration (sensitivity, support, etc.).*

4. Avoid attacking comments such as, *"You did . . ."* or *"You always . . ."*

5. If your friend responds defensively, say, *"I understand that you may not be aware of how I'm feeling. That's why I'm telling you."*

6. If your friend pleads innocent, say, *"I just want to explain how I feel to prevent a small problem from becoming a larger one."*

7. Say, *"I value our friendship and feel that it is strong enough to talk about a problem."*

8. Tell your friend that you are willing to forgive and forget. Say, *"As far as I am concerned, I've said what I wanted to say and the case is closed. I have no hard feelings."*

PART 2

INTIMATE CONVERSATIONS WITH YOUR LOVER

TURNING
A FRIEND
INTO A
LOVER

L-O-V-E. People sing about it, poets write about it, we watch movies and read books about it, and nearly everyone dreams of it! Love and sex are the most popular subjects for conversation, and everyone has an opinion about them. How to find love, how to stay in love, and how to attain a good love relationship seem to be the eternal questions. While there is no surefire formula for falling in love, experts agree that friendship plays a key role in building an intimate and long-lasting love relationship.

Dear Gabby:

I have a friend whom I am physically attracted to, but I am afraid to let my feelings show because I don't want to ruin our friendship. Is there a way to find out if my friend has any amorous feelings for me, and will I risk losing a good friendship if I try to turn it into a love relationship?

Signed,
Willing to Love

FRIENDSHIP CAN LEAD TO A LOVE RELATIONSHIP

Many single people fantasize about meeting their true love in a singles bar, an elevator, or even walking down the street. While strangers do occasionally fall in love at first sight, your chances of making a love relationship work dramatically improve if you know the person as a friend before you become romantically involved.

Rather than being frustrated in an unsociable singles bar, take a fresh look at a friend as a potential lover. Adult-education classes, recreation clubs, political groups, church groups, social organizations, the office, or work-sponsored teams are excellent places to develop friendships that can lead to romance. These situations allow two people to get to know each other in a low-risk way, and help them determine if they are interested in pursuing a more intimate relationship.

THE GREATEST FEAR IS LOSING THE FRIENDSHIP

There are risks anytime you put your feelings on the line, and seeking to turn a friend into a lover is no exception. Many people have mixed feelings about getting sexually involved with a friend because they fear that the friendship may be lost. Even so, if a friendship is strong, it can survive an unsuccessful attempt to turn it into a more intimate relationship, and if the love relationship does succeed, the friendship will continue to grow as a result of the romantic involvement. If you think that the potential for a long-term relationship is good, then consider taking the risk of seeing how the other person feels about introducing sex into the friendship.

TAKING THE PLUNGE INTO LOVE

When a person has a change in a love relationship, his other friendships may change as a result. For example, if a love relationship ends, what was only a friendship with another person can shift into a romantic relationship. Suddenly you and your friend realize you have been attracted to each other all along, but for one reason or another you have not consciously thought about it. When this situation happens you can keep your feelings secret, leaving your friendship as is. However, if you remain quiet, do not be surprised when your friend becomes involved with someone else—in which case your friendship is going to change again anyway. You can also flirt by dropping a few subtle hints that suggest you have some hidden feeling which you would like to reveal. You can say,

"How do you feel about being single again?"

"Are you dating anyone you like?"

"I'm dating too, but I haven't met anyone special. How about you?"

"I think it is hard to find the right person who can be a lover and a friend. What do you feel about friendship and love?"

You can also openly discuss how you and your friend feel about each other. You never know—your amorous desires may be mutual! You can say,

"Our friendship is very important to me, and I would never do anything to jeopardize it, but I'm feeling like there is more to our relationship than just being friends. How do you feel about that?"

"Since we've both become single again, I feel like our friendship is changing. Are you feeling that way too?"

"I want to tell you how I feel about you and I'd like to know how you feel about me. Do you want to talk about it?"

When you choose to reveal your romantic interests, either subtly or directly, you are risking the friendship as it stands with the hope that a more intimate and rewarding relationship will result. Keep in mind that just talking about your attitudes and feelings for each other does not mean either of you must make any kind of commitment.

SHOULD YOU BECOME ROMANTICALLY INVOLVED WITH YOUR FRIEND?

No one knows how a love affair will turn out, but you will have a better idea whether to commit to a romantic relationship or keep your friendship as it is if you casually discuss questions such as,

"What kind of relationship are you looking for?"

"Do you like dating more than one person at a time?"

"What is the most important thing to you in a love relationship?"

"I'd like to know how you feel about me."

HOW TO GIVE A FRIEND A 'SOFT REJECTION'

While these questions may seem blunt, studies clearly show that undefined and unfulfilled expectations are the greatest threats to a new love relationship. You can save yourself and your friend a lot of heartache by openly discussing your expectations before you make any commitment to change your friendship. After exchanging your views, if you find that you share a common outlook, then your friendship may be at a turning point for more personal involvement. However, if you do not want to get romantically involved with your friend then it is best to say so directly, but gently. You can say,

"I feel flattered that you like me as much as you do and I want you to know that I like you too, but just as a friend. I think it is best if we keep our friendship as it is."

"Even though we are good friends, I feel that our differences in style would cause us a lot of problems in a love relationship. Let's just be friends."

"I like you a lot too, but I'm not ready for a more intimate relationship right now."

"I appreciate you sharing your feelings with me. I want to be honest with you too. I'd prefer it if we would just remain friends for the time being."

HOW TO HANDLE A REJECTION

Dear Gabby:

My friend doesn't want to get romantically involved with me. Will our friendship ever be the same?

Signed,
Rejected

There is no question that being rejected by a friend is painful, but keep in mind that being turned down as a lover does not mean that the friendship is over. In addition to not wanting to risk the friendship, there may be other reasons for the rejection, including poor timing, fear of commitment, or fear of intimacy. For example, perhaps your friend is still recovering from a past romance that went sour, from a divorce, or even from the loss of his or her spouse, and is simply not ready for a new emotional attachment.

Quickly bouncing back from the rejection and letting your friend know that you respect his or her decision without any hard feelings is the key to getting your friendship back on track. Sulking, getting angry, or pressuring your friend into an intimate commitment that he or she does not want, or is not ready for, often produces the opposite results. It is better to keep your conversation low-key and casual, but honest. You can say,

*"I appreciate your honesty, even though it is not the answer
I wanted to hear. In any case, I still want to be friends."*

*"I just wanted to tell you how I feel about you, but I accept
your decision. I hope we can still be friends because I never
want that to change."*

FROM FRIENDS TO LOVERS:
REDEFINING EXPECTATIONS AND
COMMITMENT

Dear Gabby:

*I had an affair with a friend and she wanted a long-
term relationship with me, but I didn't want to make
a commitment. She got very angry with me and our
friendship went right down the drain. What went
wrong?*

Signed,
Confused Lover

Caution! Lovers with radically different expectations,
especially concerning future commitment and intimacy,
will often end up with wounded pride and a damaged
friendship. If one friend is only after some fun in bed
while the other is looking for true commitment, then
both the friendship and love affair are in jeopardy.

Even if you do make a mutual commitment, the
change in your level of intimacy may be disruptive to
your friendship. For example, when you were just
friends, perhaps it was easier to discuss sensitive issues
because you were not sexually involved. Now that the
relationship has changed, you may feel more inhibited

expressing your feelings than before. This is where the need for intimate conversations is crucial.

Although candidly talking about personal issues such as sex, intimacy, commitment, and expectations may be difficult at first, if you want your love affair and friendship to flourish at the same time, intimate communication is a must. Frequent and honest discussions indicate trust, and as a result they encourage greater intimacy in your relationship. But intimate conversations do more than help you get to know your lover better—they also allow you to overcome the many hurdles that every couple faces as their love affair develops into a lasting partnership. Here are some intimate conversation starters:

"Can we talk about the changes our relationship is going through?"

"I want to know how you are feeling about our friendship. Have your feelings changed?"

"How do you feel about our new relationship? Are you happy with the changes?"

"Do you have any regrets about getting more intimately involved?"

"What do you see for the future of our relationship? Commitment is important to me. How do you feel about commitment?"

"I want you to know that I am the happiest I've been in a long time. I feel great when I'm with you! How are you feeling about me?"

ESTABLISH A PATTERN OF INTIMATE CONVERSATIONS

Falling in love is one thing, but staying in love is something else. The conversation patterns you establish early on will be the foundation upon which the rest of your relationship is based. Keep in mind that once poor communication habits are established, they are difficult to alter without hard work and, many times, bruised feelings. On the other hand, if you sincerely and openly talk about sex, passion, commitment, and intimacy from the very beginning, then your love affair has a good chance of growing into a long-lasting love relationship.

GABBY GABOR'S CONVERSATION CLINIC #5

HOW TO BE YOUR LOVER'S BEST FRIEND

Intimate conversations are more than just communicating about sex and your relationship, but also include talking about everyday activities, feelings, hopes, and dreams. Being intimate is more than just showing passion—it is showing that you care enough to be your lover's best friend.

What to Do	What to Say
Show an interest in your lover's work or hobby.	*"How was your job interview (club meeting, class, etc.)?"*
Encourage conversations about fantasies and dreams.	*"If you could do anything in the world you wanted, what would it be?"*
Demonstrate cooperation by going the extra mile.	*"Let me know if there is anything I can do to help you."*

Give confidence-building feedback.	*"That is a beautiful job! You sure have come a long way!"*
Be your lover's biggest fan.	*"I think you are the greatest!"*
Make your lover's day.	*"You are looking great today!"*
Build your lover's self-esteem.	*"You are the sunshine of my life!"*
Say the magic words.	*"I love you more than anyone else in the world!"*

PATCHING UP A
LOVERS' QUARREL

"When my lover and I first got together our relationship was great, but now all we do is fight over stupid things like who does the dishes or pays for dinner."

Do you and your lover constantly argue but never resolve your differences? Are your exchanges filled with hostile accusations that leave both of you frustrated and angry? Do you feel like your relationship resembles a wild roller-coaster ride more than a trip through the tunnel of love?

As new lovers spend more time together their differences can lead to spats or even knock-down, drag-out fights. Minor irritations, disagreements, or conflicting lifestyles that seem unimportant in the beginning of their relationship can become serious sources of discord that may turn a passionate love affair sour. What began as infatuation and affection is soon displaced by animosity and conflict, which saps intimacy and love from the relationship.

A decline in a love relationship rarely happens all at once, but rather takes place between cycles of *"Things are going great"* and *"We're not getting along too well right now."* Continuous emotional upheavals, even with the occasional respite, are frustrating, and if the disputes cannot be satisfactorily resolved, they may ultimately lead to the demise of the relationship.

HOW DO YOU AND YOUR LOVER DEAL WITH DAY-TO-DAY CONFLICT?

Nearly every love relationship experiences ups and downs at various times, but most experts agree that how a couple deals with day-to-day emotional conflict plays an important role in determining the success or failure of their partnership.

People react to anger in various ways. Shy individuals often hide their discontent or express it indirectly with long silent periods, slamming doors, storming off, sar-

castic comments, or withholding affection. Hidden anger confuses and compounds the original problem so that it becomes increasingly difficult to pinpoint the trouble spot and to talk it through to a satisfactory solution.

While some people keep their anger bottled up inside, others go to the opposite extreme and ventilate their frustrations as if their lovers are impervious to pain. If you think that dumping anger on your lover is a constructive way to relieve stress, and that afterward your problems will disappear, then think again! Contrary to this popular belief, hostile outbursts that brutalize one person's feelings tend to aggravate problems, lead to more volatile behavior, and frequently hasten the demise of the relationship.

UNDEFINED ANGER CAUSES ARGUMENTS

"*That's not what I mean, but I just can't explain it!*"

When a person is upset and frustrated it is difficult to communicate effectively. But is it realistic to expect your lover to understand why you are upset if you cannot clearly express yourself? If you simply get angry without specifically defining the problem, then you may be setting the stage for an emotional war of words with angry counteraccusations. Keep in mind that undefined frustrations create more misunderstanding, hurt feelings, and antagonism.

Instead of screaming heated accusations—such as "This is all your fault!" *"Don't you ever do anything right?"* or *"How could you be so stupid?"*—clearly describe the specific reasons why you are unhappy. As best you can, calmly present your views without being re-

How do you respond when differences arise between you and your lover? Are you unassertive or assertive?

Unassertive	Assertive
Communicate your displeasure with the "silent treatment."	*Calmly explain why you are upset.*
Clam up in frustration and hope that a problem will go away.	*Discuss conflicts openly as they arise.*
Blow up when your lover fails to fulfill your unstated or implied wishes.	*Explain your expectations.*
Express your anger through sarcastic remarks, withdrawing, or withholding affection.	*Use the words, "I'm angry!"*
Become defensive if your lover criticizes you.	*Listen and admit your mistakes.*
Blame your lover for your problems.	*Take responsibility and seek solutions.*
Hold a grudge and refuse to make reasonable changes.	*Compromise, forgive, apologize, and try to do better next time.*

duced to tears, shouting, or dramatic gestures to make your lover understand. To express your anger you can say,

"I am upset and angry because . . ."

"I am disappointed because . . ."

"I feel let down because . . ."

"I am unhappy because . . ."

"I don't feel that I am being treated right because . . ."

NIPPING MINOR IRRITATIONS IN THE BUD

Since many full-blown arguments grow out of minor irritations, one good strategy is to talk about them before they escalate into a verbal war. To organize your thoughts and feelings, divide a sheet of paper into two columns and take an inventory of what is bothering you. Then write down the words that best express how you feel about the situation and what you want your lover to do. Here is an example:

The Problem	How to Say It
My lover never helps me with the chores.	*"I'm overloaded with housework. I need you to help me."*
My lover wants me to discipline the kids as soon as I get home.	*"Let's discuss our strategy about the kids after I relax for a few minutes."*

My lover never asks me how my day was.	*"I had an interesting day. Do you want to hear about it?"*
My lover asks about my day but I just want to forget about it.	*"I'd rather not talk about it just now. How was your day?"*
My lover is always so busy with the kids we never get a chance to be alone.	*"Let's put the kids to bed early tonight so we can spend some time together alone."*

This strategy helps create effective communication in three ways. First, writing your specific complaints will help you pinpoint trouble areas and eliminate confusing and accusatory statements. Second, writing what you want to say helps you find the right words to best express yourself. Finally, writing allows you to review what you want to say before you say it, thus avoiding inflammatory remarks or criticisms, which can spark defensiveness, hostility, or a major confrontation.

Note: While it is okay to write any words to sort out your feelings, avoid using the phrases *"You should . . . ," "You shouldn't . . . ,"* or *"Don't you think that . . . ?"* when presenting your views.

BE DIRECT AND HONEST

"**I** *want you to know how I am feeling about . . ."*

To express anger effectively, use words that reflect your gut feelings, such as *happy, sad, love, hate, afraid, joy, concern, disappointed, expect, hope,* and so on. Avoid formal language, longwinded personal philosophy, or judgmental statements. Instead of being outwardly angry, collect yourself. Be as calm, confident, and in control of your emotions as possible. You can say,

"I feel sad that we are drifting apart and I am disappointed that we are not getting along as well as we once did."

"I'm unhappy with the direction our relationship is going and I hope that we can change that."

"I'm afraid that if we don't resolve some outstanding problems soon, our relationship may not last and that concerns me."

"I don't want to argue. I want to talk about our problems so we can reach some compromise solutions."

"I want to know how you are feeling about our relationship."

Dear Gabby:

My boyfriend and I have fun together most of the time, but sometimes he loses his temper at my most innocent comment. I feel very uncomfortable because I never know what's going to set him off. How can I calm him down and find out why he gets so mad?

Signed,
Walking on Eggs

If a lover is so unpredictable that you never know when he will fly into a rage, then his anger is just below the surface, waiting for a convenient excuse to blow. If you sense that he wants to open up, you might encourage him before he loses his temper by asking, *"How are you feeling today?" "Is something bothering you?"* If he does erupt after a seemingly innocent comment or question, you can say, *"What is it about what I have said that upsets you so much? Please tell me. If I said something that hurt your feelings or offended you, I apologize, but it sounds like something else is bothering you. What is it? Let's quietly talk about it."*

Be aware, however, that your "innocent comment" may be interpreted as judgmental or as a veiled criticism. If this is the case, then your boyfriend may be reacting to what he perceives as your disapproval or manipulation.

DEFUSING AN ARGUMENT

There are constructive ways to express anger that fall somewhere between remaining passively silent and letting it burst in a fit of uncontrollable rage. If you start to lose your temper, get control of your emotions by asking yourself:

- How angry am I on a scale of one to ten, ten being the most angry?

- Why am I upset? What are the specific reasons?

- Am I overreacting to constructive criticism?

- Am I misinterpreting friendly teasing as a personal attack?

- Am I losing my sense of humor?

- Am I jumping to the wrong conclusion?

- Is there something else bothering me that I have not openly talked about?

If you determine that you have good reason for being upset with your lover, it is best to release your anger in a controlled manner. Take a moment to regain your composure, even if the other person is doing his best to get your goat. Keep in mind that if you give your lover a piece of your mind, chances are you have lost control and you may say words that you will later regret. Consider calling time out to reevaluate the situation and to let tempers cool down. To curb hostilities and clear up misunderstandings before they do irrevocable damage to your relationship, you can say,

"I'm not sure what you mean. Perhaps I misunderstood what you are saying. Can we start again?"

"I'm upset and angry, but I want to think about what you have said before I respond."

"I am reacting to an issue that needs to be resolved by both of us working together."

"Let's sit down when we both are calm, quietly talk about the problem, and try to reach a compromise solution."

TAKE A STEP BACK FROM THE CONFLICT

It is difficult to remain cool and calm in a quarrel, especially if you must endure hostile accusations or personal attacks. But it is better to walk away from a heated argument with your lover rather than think that you must win by losing your temper or fighting it out to the bitter end. Consider doing some physical activity such as jogging or taking a long walk to release the tension and frustration while you sort out your feelings and options. Once you are one step removed from the conflict, it will be easier to get a clearer view of the specific problems affecting your relationship and come up with some possible solutions.

SERIOUS PROBLEMS NEED ONGOING DISCUSSIONS

When lovers withdraw from an argument their anger may temporarily subside, but the couple's intimacy may suffer. If, however, you agree to discuss the issues coolly, then the anger can fade away naturally without diminishing how you and your partner feel about each other. It is important to note that frequent discussions are the best way to solve serious disagreements. Even so, you can get off the day-to-day emotional roller coaster if you resolve minor problems before they escalate out of control and ruin your relationship for good. If you cannot agree to sit down and talk, or there seems to be little or no movement toward a satisfactory resolution, then you may want to seek professional counseling before you reach the point of calling it quits.

Admitting the real reasons for frustration and displeasure in a relationship and doing something about them is difficult, but definitely worthwhile. Keep in mind that calmly expressing anger will not necessarily solve all your troubles, but if you and your lover are willing to directly face the issues, sincerely speak your mind, and agree to find compromise solutions that work, then you can use your anger to improve and strengthen your love relationship. As you zero in on concrete reasons why you are angry, finding solutions is much easier. In this way intimate conversations become an effective strategy of assertive and gentle confrontation which can bring you and your lover a happier and more loving relationship.

GABBY GABOR'S
CONVERSATION CLINIC #6
MAKING UP WITH YOUR LOVER

*C*reate an atmosphere for ending a quarrel by showing a willingness to openly talk about conflicting issues. Make it a point to listen carefully to your lover's point of view and be willing to say, "I understand how you feel. I made a mistake and I apologize. I'll work harder on doing better. Let's make up."

---

1. Agree: *"Arguing is ruining our relationship. Let's find a better way to communicate."*

2. Acknowledge and agree: *"Both of our feelings are important. We both make mistakes. We can both make some changes."*

3. Ask: *"Which specific problems do you feel need immediate attention?"*

4. Suggest: *"Let's write down areas where we agree and disagree. Then let's discuss possible compromises where we have different viewpoints."*

5. Agree: *"Let's find a few points that we can resolve even if they seem minor."*

6. Offer to compromise by saying: *"What would you like me to do differently?"*

7. **Discuss:** *"What do we want from each other and our relationship?"*

8. **Acknowledge:** *"I understand your point of view better than I did before and I want this relationship to work."*

9. **Acknowledge and agree:** *"I'm glad we sat down and talked this problem out—I feel much better. Let's sit down and talk again tomorrow."*

10. **Acknowledge that a satisfactory solution was reached and say:** *"I'm not angry anymore. I love you. Are you still angry? Do you still love me?"*

INTIMATE

CONVERSATIONS

ABOUT SEX

Sex, sex, sex, and more sex! Some people can never get enough while others are more interested in going shopping or watching sports on television. No matter how people feel about sex, studies show that talking about sexual topics, whether it be about the frequency of lovemaking or experimentation, is difficult—especially between lovers. As a result, much of the sexual communication between couples is expressed either nonverbally or in a subtle, private language. Nevertheless, most couples do talk about sexual topics at one time or another. Since most people's self-esteem and sexuality are closely tied, such intimate conversations should always be approached sensitively.

Sex is always an emotionally charged subject, so keep in mind that criticism is hurtful and can quickly de-

crease intimacy in your relationship. On the other hand, playful teasing, warm touches, gentle experimentation, and honest communication are good ways to express your sexual desires. When you openly talk about sex, the intimacy in your relationship will increase, and so will the quality of your sex life.

DO'S AND DON'TS WHEN TALKING ABOUT SEX

D o tell your lover that he or she turns you on.

Every lover wants to hear that he or she is attractive and has sex appeal. Even if you have been a couple for years, don't neglect your partner's desire to hear the words, *"You are one sexy man (woman)."*

D o n ' t assume that having sex is the only form of intimacy.

No matter how often a couple makes love, the quality of their relationship is directly related to their level of intimate communication. Therefore, it is vital to reveal your intimate feelings verbally as well as physically. To be more intimate you reaffirm your feelings of love and closeness. For example, you can say, *"I want you to know that I love you more than anyone or anything in the whole world. My life would be empty without you. I just love being with you. Meeting you was the greatest thing that ever happened to me. I am the luckiest person in the world to be with you."*

D o let your lover know that you are in the mood for love.

Many lovers are shy about expressing their desire to make love because they fear rejection. While hearing *"I have a headache"* can be disappointing, fear of rejection can paralyze and ruin your sex life. Therefore, take the risk and lightheartedly say, *"Hey sweetie, do you wanna have some fun in bed tonight?"*

D o n ' t compare your spouse with a past lover.

Making comparisons between lovers past and present is insensitive as well as bad strategy if improving your sex life is the goal. Past lovers whose favors you once enjoyed are of better use in your fantasies than as part of your conversations with your present lover. So *don't* say, *"My ex-lover loved sex. Why don't you?"*

D o test your partner's mood before you make strong sexual advances.

A little nibble on the neck, kiss on the ear, or rub on

the behind are typical signals of sexual desire. If, however, your overtures are not returned in kind, then you may be seeing a signal that suggests "Not tonight dear." Rather than force the sexual issue right away, show your spouse some intimate, yet nonsexual physical attention. For example, you can say, *"I can tell you are a little tense. How about a nice backrub?"* Then take another reading and see how he or she feels about making love by saying, *"How are you feeling now?"*

D o n ' t give your spouse a cold rejection.

Harsh sexual rejections are hurtful and embarrassing. They tend to make the rejected lover shy, and ultimately can sap intimacy from a relationship. If you are not in the mood to make love, then you can say, *"I'm really not in the mood. I wish I had a little more energy for you tonight, but all I want to do now is close my eyes and go to sleep."* Then give your lover a warm hug and kiss and say, *"I love you!"*

D o tell your lover that you want to make love soon.

Even if you are not ready for a round of lovemaking, tell your lover that it is the time or situation that is standing in the way, not him or her. Then say, *"I'm looking forward to the weekend so we can spend some extra time in bed."*

D o n ' t talk about a sexual problem while you are in bed or having sex.

Discussing a sexual dysfunction or disappointment in bed as it happens is demoralizing and can complicate the problem. A better strategy is to say, *"Don't worry about it. It's not that important. I still love you. We can talk about it later."* Then choose a nonsexual time, such as after breakfast, to discuss the problem without the added pressure to perform sexually.

D o show a willingness to talk about a sexual problem.

If a couple has sexual problems, then discussing them privately is the first step to finding a solution. This is probably one of the most difficult conversations there is, so extra sensitivity is necessary if your spouse is to be receptive. You can say, *"You know that I love you very much and I know that you love me. We both know that our sex life needs some improvement. I want to talk about what we can do. How do you feel about discussing it?"*

D o n ' t assume that a sexual problem cannot be solved.

While chronic sexual problems usually require professional therapy, many sexual difficulties can be overcome with patience, sensitivity, and understanding when discussing sexual feelings and insecurities. You can say, *"I have insecure feelings and hang-ups about sex too. Let's talk about our feelings and maybe we can understand each other better. That certainly can't hurt our sex life!"*

D o vary your sexual routine to increase spontaneity.

Most couples have passionate sex in the beginning of their relationship. As time goes on, the passion may die down and the partners settle into a sexual timetable that can become routine. To break out of a sexual routine you can suggest, *"How about a romantic lunch and a little afternoon romp?"*

D o n ' t assume that your lover knows what you like best about your sex life.

Partners expect a lot from each other, sometimes assuming one another to be mind readers. However, when it comes to sex, many people are too embarrassed or shy to say what they like or want. An easy way to express your sexual preferences is to say, *"I love it when you . . ."* To ask your lover about his or her sexual preferences you can say, *"What do you like best when we make love?"*

D o be open to experimentation to add spice to your sex life.

While many people are embarrassed discussing sex, many other couples find that talking about sex is stimulating. If there is a particular sexual technique that you would like to bring into your relationship, then suggest the idea in a way that is inviting and arousing, not threatening. You can say, *"Have you ever wanted to . . . ? I've always wanted to . . . , but I never have. Are you willing to give it a try?"*

D o n ' t pry too deeply into your lover's past sexual relationships.

Tempting as it may be, asking too-personal questions about past sexual escapades may lead you into areas you will find disconcerting. If your lover asks you a question that you would rather not answer, you can tell a little white lie by saying, *"Oh that happened so long ago I don't remember the details."*

D o say these three magic words often: *"I love you!"*

LITTLE SEXUAL INTIMACIES MEAN A LOT

Most lovers like the little touches, affectionate compliments, and subtle words that show their partner's continued sexual interest. Talking about sex is almost as much fun as having sex—but not quite! So with or without being explicit, let your sexual feelings show, be willing to say how you feel and what you want. In other words, have an intimate conversation about sex! Then see what happens! Chances are, you and your lover will have a lot more fun in bed!

GABBY GABOR'S CONVERSATION CLINIC #7

BREAKING THROUGH THE INTIMACY BARRIER

Men and women frequently define intimacy differently. Women say that when men are more open with their feelings the couple's intimacy increases. Men, on the other hand, suggest that intimacy increases when they share more activities with their partner. Whether you're a man or woman, the best way to build intimacy in your relationship is to be more open about your feelings and spend more time with your lover. Try these conversation-starters with your partner and watch intimacy grow in your relationship.

1. **Say something you like about your relationship.** For example, *"I feel happy being with you because . . ."* or *"I really enjoy being with you because you make me feel so good."*

2. **Reveal some personal information about yourself.** For example, *"I want to tell you something about myself that I've never mentioned to you before,"* or *"There is something personal that I want to share with you."*

3. Show that you are willing to be more open by following up an intimate conversation with some additional insights into your private world. You might say, *"I'd like to talk more about what we were discussing the other evening,"* or *"I've never told anyone this before, but . . ."*

4. Encourage intimate conversation by being a nonjudgmental listener. Try saying, *"If there is something bothering you and you want to talk about it, I'm willing to listen,"* or *"How are you feeling about our sex life now?"*

5. Express your desire to be more intimate by suggesting enjoyable activities which the two of you can share together. You can say, *"I want to do more fun things together. Would you like to go on a picnic this weekend?"* or *"How about just the two of us taking off for a romantic weekend?"*

6. Be available to talk over problems with your mate, offer advice, provide encouragement or assistance, and offer moral support. You can say, *"I know that you've been having a tough time recently and I want you to know that if there is anything I can do to help you or if you just want to talk about it, I'm here."*

7. Always tell your partner how much you appreciate him or her. Say, *"I want you to know that I really appreciate all the things you do for me. You're terrific!"*

8. Look for small increases in intimacy and let your lover know that you like what you see. You can say, *"I really like the way we are communicating now. I feel closer to you than I ever have before and that really makes me feel good."*

PART
3

INTIMATE CONVERSATIONS WITH YOUR FAMILY

BOOSTING YOUR CHILD'S CONFIDENCE AND SELF-ESTEEM

"*I have been shy all my life. I just wish my parents had encouraged me to talk more as a kid.*"

Is your child shy, timid, or lacking in confidence? Although many young people eventually grow more confident as they mature, others suffer from shyness throughout their adult lives. As a parent, you can help build your child's confidence and self-esteen by using the following conversational techniques. Not only will these tips help your child overcome shyness and provide confidence to succeed, but they will create a communication channel from which everyone in your family can benefit.

Each letter in the word *F-R-I-E-N-D-S* represents a conversational technique for helping a child overcome shyness and build confidence.

F = Friendly Mood
R = Respectful Attitude
I = Interested Listening
E = Enthusiasm
N = Nurturing
D = Dialogue with Your Child
S = Self-Esteem and Confidence

F STANDS FOR FRIENDLY MOOD

The power of a friendly adult can do more for a child's confidence than many parents might imagine. Creating a comfortable atmosphere conducive to conversations helps overcome shyness because your child will feel more receptive and less defensive. Therefore, rather than immediately challenging your kid about sloppy homework, neglected chores, or coming home late, you will achieve far greater results if you smile, give her a friendly hello, a compliment, or a question which encourages conversation. Try these approaches to show your child that you are in a friendly mood:

• Be optimistic and upbeat by saying,

"Good morning! You're looking good today. I like your outfit (hair, shoes, shirt, etc.)."

"What a gorgeous day! How about joining me for a quick jog around the block (walk with the dog, game of tennis, etc.)?"

- Show you are open and receptive to conversation by saying,

"Hi, how are you? Did you have a good day in school (at work, your father's house, etc.)?"

"Tell me about your day. How's it going?"

"You must be happy the weekend is here. Is there anything special that you would like to do?"

- Share your sense of humor and laugh with your child by saying something like,

"Gee, I worked so hard today that my brain is going to melt! How are you feeling tonight?"

"Say, I heard a funny joke today. Want to hear it?"

"I really got a chuckle out of that story you wrote. You've got a great sense of humor. I'd love to read another one. I need a lift!"

"Did you read this morning's comics? They are a riot!"

"That movie we watched last night was funny. I especially like the part where . . . Did you enjoy it? What part did you like best?"

R STANDS FOR RESPECTFUL ATTITUDE

Mutual respect is at the basis of every productive relationship and is an essential building block for a child's confidence and self-esteem. Most parents want their children to be obedient, polite, kind, and considerate of others, yet many fail to treat their kids with the respect that they demand in return. When children are treated with respect, they learn its value, thus gaining self-respect and confidence, as well as a willingness to treat others similarly. To foster a respectful attitude in your child, try these suggestions:

- When you ask your child to do something for you, always show the kind of courtesy that you expect from him or her in return. Include the words, *please* and *thank you.* Say,

"Would you mind helping me for a minute or two? I would appreciate it if you would . . ."

- Accept your child's opinions, even though they may differ from yours. This shows that you respect his or her right to think differently than you. Say,

"I respect your opinion even though I do not agree with it, but you have the right to think what you want."

- Acknowledge your child's right to disagree, even though you retain the authority to make a final decision. Say,

"I understand that you disagree with me and that's your right, but since I'm your mother (father, stepparent, guardian, etc.) I reserve the right to say yes or no."

- Since decision-making is a learned process, allow your child the opportunity to make some personal decisions. Say,

"If you want to quit your dance lessons, that is your choice. I'd like to see you continue, but it is up to you."

• Increase your child's confidence by giving her more independence as she demonstrates an ability to handle greater responsibility. You can say,

"You've proven to me that you can handle responsibility, so you can borrow the car (stay out later, go camping, etc.)."

I STANDS FOR INTERESTED LISTENING

Many parents tell their child what to do, when to do it, and even what to think! While it is necessary to check up on your kid's homework assignments, chores, or other unfinished business, if you first take a few minutes to ask about and listen to what is exciting in his life, then he will have the opportunity to put shyness aside and talk to you. Here are some ways to show interest:

• Ask questions about the important aspects of your child's life. For example,

"Tell me, how did your baseball practice (dance class, cheerleading practice, drama rehearsal, etc.) go this afternoon? Are you enjoying it? What do you like best about it?"

"What are the other kids like in your class? Did you meet any new friends? What are your teachers like?"

"How is your airplane model (sewing project, clubhouse, etc.) coming along? Give me an update."

While yes-no or short-answer questions are good conversation-starters, without enthusiastic and open-ended follow-up questions that encourage a more detailed response, your conversations may not get the boost they need to really get going. *"What do you think or feel about . . . ?"* questions demonstrate that you are willing to listen and are interested in your child's thoughts, feelings, and opinions. Here are ways to encourage your child to elaborate on his or her topics of interest:

- To show you are listening and want to continue talking about a particular topic, restate what he or she has said in a few words and then ask open-ended follow-up questions. You can say,

"It sounds like you had a great time at the swimming pool today. What is it about going to the swimming pool that you like best?"

"I'm glad you are enjoying the play you are in. Have you ever wondered what it would be like to be a professional actress?"

- If your child is old enough to participate in family decisions, ask for an opinion or for advice concerning a situation you face, or a question you have. You can say,

"I'd like to ask you your opinion on something. I'm debating how I should approach this situation. What do you think would be best for our family?"

"I'm interested in your opinion about . . ."

"I'd be interested to know how you would handle the situation."

- To encourage a continued dialogue about a subject even if you disagree with your kid's viewpoint, listen carefully without interruption or criticism. Then focus on the points you more or less agree with, even if the thrust of his or her opinion is contrary to yours. You can say,

"Thanks for sharing your ideas with me."

"Although I don't agree with everything you've said, there are some points that we agree on."

"I'm going to think carefully about what you have said. You have a good head on your shoulders! I respect your opinion."

Note: Take care not to burden your child with your adult responsibilities or expect him or her to solve your problems. If you overemphasize your need for a solution, your child may feel responsible if things go wrong, or worry about a situation that is beyond his or her control.

E STANDS FOR ENTHUSIASM

Everyone knows that enthusiasm is catchy. As you and your child share each other's passion for sports, cooking, gardening, model-making, sewing, music, or computers, your conversations will be directed to topics you can both enjoy and participate in together. As a result, you will foster a confidence-building environment in which you can comfortably converse without disciplining, lecturing or nagging. To share your enthusiasm for a hobby or interest, try this approach:

- Show your child that you want to spend time together by inviting him or her to join you in an activity that you both enjoy. You can say,

"There is a new car (boat, computer, motorcycle, fabric, art, etc.) show at the convention center. I'm excited about going. Would you like to join me?"

"I just read the most delicious-sounding dessert recipe. I don't have anything planned for this rainy afternoon and it might be fun to try it out. Do you want to help me?"

- Show that you are open to learning new things and want to spend time together by expressing enthusiasm for your child's hobby or special interest. You can say,

"That computer chess game you taught me is a lot of fun. I never thought I could do that kind of thing. What do you say we play it again?"

"I've always wanted to learn how to play the guitar and you play like a pro. Can you give me a few tips?"

N STANDS FOR NURTURING

Children need nurturing because the world is a fascinating, yet scary place to grow up in. Allowing children to explore their surroundings at a comfortable rate builds confidence and self-esteem. Some parents, while their intentions may be good, insist on helping their children too much, leaving them with little opportunity to gain the confidence and experience necessary to face future challenges. On the other hand, if a parent assists too little, the child will miss needed praise, encouragement, and guidance. But when a parent provides *measured* guidance and praise, children become enthusiastic about discovery and learning. Nurturing your child as you talk, work, and play together is an excellent way to boost confidence and self-esteem. Here are some suggestions:

- Keep your child's self-confidence growing by always praising even the smallest accomplishments—what appears to be a minor task to you could be a big step forward for your kid. You can say, *"Good job! Well done! Nice going! Now you've got the right idea!"* Then just watch your kid's face light up!

- To build your child's ability to start and finish projects, give him or her the opportunity to take charge of a task that you do together, but let your child progress at his or her own rate. You can say,

"Okay, you're the boss. What do we do first? Now, what's next? It's up to you."

"How will we know when the job is finished?"

Similarly, help your child learn to solve problems by being patient and allowing time for him to discover an answer or solution, rather than showing him how to do it. Encourage your child to experiment to find a solution. You can say,

"There is more than one way to do most things. Take your time and think this out one step at a time. Then give it another try and see what you come up with."

"It is okay to make mistakes. That is how we learn."

- Encourage your child's best effort without over-emphasizing competition. You can say,

"Doing your best means to challenge yourself. See what you can do when you try your hardest. You will feel satisfied— and good about yourself—so long as you're doing the best you can."

"Just do your best and don't worry about how well anyone else does. What is most important is giving the job your best effort."

• To encourage your child to finish a difficult task, emphasize that perseverance is one of the keys to success and confidence. You can say,

"Remember the proverb, 'If at first you don't succeed, then try, try again.' "

"Don't worry if you don't succeed the first time, second time, or even the third time. Just keep at it, and you'll get what you want. That is called perseverance—and perseverance pays off!"

• To show that you have faith in your child's abilities, praise his or her efforts. You can say,

"Congratulations. You did it all by yourself! Now that is an accomplishment to be proud of!"

"I'm proud that you kept working at it, even when the going got tough!"

"You really know the meaning of perseverance. I'm proud of you!"

D STANDS FOR DIALOGUE WITH YOUR CHILD

Many parents complain that their children do not listen to them. Likewise, kids say that their parents do not understand them. This communication breakdown not only causes family conflict, but it also saps a child's confidence and self-esteem, and increases shyness. Try these suggestions for opening and maintaining a dialogue with your child.

• Keep in touch with your child's feelings by monitoring her emotional state. You can say,

"How are you feeling about moving to a new city (taking your final exam, your new baby brother, going out on your first date, etc.)?"

• Avert unexpected blowups or fights by gently confronting minor problems before they get out of hand. You can say,

"I'm concerned that you've been upset (not eating, argumentative, hostile, etc.) lately. What's the trouble?"

"Believe it or not, I was once your age too and I know it can get tough sometimes! Maybe I can help. Would you like to talk about it?"

• Keep minor incidents from growing into major conflicts by quickly clearing up misunderstandings as they arise. You can say,

"I want to apologize for losing my temper with you yesterday. I didn't understand that you had already finished your homework (had completed your chores, were not responsible for breaking the lamp, etc.)."

"It was my mistake to assume that you were just goofing off. Sorry. I'll be more patient next time."

•   Keep the communication channels open by foster-
ing an environment of trust and love. You can say,

*"There is something personal that I want to talk with you
about."*

*"I want you to know that if you ever want to talk to me about
anything at all I'm always willing to sit down and listen. You
know that I love you very much."*

*"Sometimes life gets pretty confusing, but talking with peo-
ple you trust can help. I'm always here when you want to
talk."*

*"If you have done something that you are ashamed of or that
you think I will be angry about, tell me. If you are honest
and up-front with me I can be a lot more understanding than
you might think—plus I probably won't be as mad if you tell
me about something that you have done, instead of waiting
for me to find out about it on my own."*

Establishing a dialogue with your child will decrease
shyness and any feelings of isolation because it takes
away the fear that many kids have of opening up to their
parents. As your child's ability to confidently communicate improves, it will enhance your relationship, build
his or her self-esteem, and promote your family's unity.

S STANDS FOR SELF-ESTEEM AND CONFIDENCE

You can promote your child's self-esteem and confidence
by acknowledging and building on his special abilities,
be they technical, artistic, or personal skills. On the
other hand, if you are overcritical, have unrealistic ex-

pectations, or do not recognize your child's talents as important, you will undermine his or her self-worth. The following suggestions will make your child feel like you appreciate him or her as an individual with something to offer.

- Build your child's self-esteem by saying that you value his or her abilities. You can say,

"You have a real talent for . . ."

"I admire your ability to keep things in order (tell a story, build furniture, etc.)."

- Build your child's confidence by acknowledging what your child is good at. You can say,

"You can draw a horse (bake a cake, play hockey, make people laugh, etc.) better than anyone I know!"

"You are the most creative person I know. How do you come up with all those nifty ideas?"

"How did you learn how to be so good at . . . ?"

- Acknowledge your child's value to others by saying,

"Not everyone can do what you do, and that is what makes you special."

"It's people like you who make life interesting."

"I bet you could be a professional . . . if you wanted to."

BREAKING THE CYCLE OF FAILURE AND LOW SELF-ESTEEM

"I can, but I won't.

I won't, so I don't.

I don't, so I can't.

I can't, but I'll say I won't."

—From the desk of Lucille Rhodes, director of the Robert Louis Stevenson School, a coeducational junior and senior high school for promising adolescents with unrealized promise.

Dear Gabby:

My teenager scores very high on intelligence tests, but he hates school and does poorly in every subject except art. I nag him constantly, but it doesn't do any good. What can I say to get him to do better in school?

Signed,
Parent of Underachiever

Many anxious parents, though their intentions may be good, undercut their child's self-esteem and confidence, thus perpetuating underachievement and failure. While breaking this cycle is difficult, parents can help if they avoid three common pitfalls.

PITFALL #1: EXCESSIVE CORRECTING AND NOT ENOUGH COMPLIMENTING

Underachievers are children who do not perform, particularly in school, up to their potential. Parents of under-

achievers spend 90 percent of the time correcting their child's behavior and only 10 percent of the time complimenting it. This reinforces undesirable behavior, ignores or minimizes desirable behavior, and saps a child's confidence and self-esteem. Many parents inadvertently criticize their kids by "sandwiching" a compliment with a negative question such as, *"You look nice today. Why can't you look like that more often?"* This double-edged comment makes your teenager feel like you are just setting her up for more criticism. Therefore, what was intended as a compliment is interpreted as a putdown, leaving the child hurt, often spiteful, and unreceptive.

A MORE EFFECTIVE APPROACH

Justifiable praise, or "stroking"—free of criticism—reinforces a child's strengths and desirable behavior, as well as building self-esteem and making him feel more open to suggestions a parent may offer. Stroking and complimenting your child is a way of saying "I like you and I think you have something to offer. You are a worthwhile person." Make your compliments simple and sincere, without attaching them to a critical comment. Since people often have difficulty accepting a compliment, follow it up with an easy-to-answer question. For example, you can say,

"You look great in your new red shirt! What other outfits could you wear it with?"

"I think you have a lot of artistic talent. What kind of artwork do you like doing best? Have you ever thought of becoming a professional?"

"I liked the way you helped that lost little boy find his mother at the fair yesterday. You showed me you know how to take charge of a situation. That was good! What made you decide to get involved and help?"

SIXTY SECONDS OF SPECIFIC PRAISE PAYS OFF

You may be surprised to know how much children value even small amounts of praise from parents or teachers. Adult praise is a useful tool in modifying a child's behavior, because it identifies desirable actions while expressing approval. When you praise your child's acceptable behavior he will be likely to repeat it with the hopes of being praised again. So, rather than harping on the old problems, try short, frequent periods of praise. Chances are, you will begin to see more of the behavior you want and less of the behavior you wish to discourage. For example, you can say,

"Billy, I just want to tell you that I think your study habits have improved since your last report card. I can see that you are trying harder and it is really paying off. I'm proud of you! Keep up the good work!"

PITFALL #2: EXCESSIVE AUTHORITY WITHOUT CONSISTENCY OR FLEXIBILITY

Parents of underachievers often make desperate attempts to exercise unrealistic or excessive authority over all aspects of their child's life (such as homework, chores, sex life, social life, career choices, free time, and so on), but lack the ability to enforce their randomly imposed rules. As a result, instead of having total control, they have little or no effect on their child's behavior. The parent who attempts to control everything usually ends up controlling nothing.

A MORE EFFECTIVE APPROACH

Acknowledge that, as a parent, you have power only in certain, but not all, areas of your child's life, and make a point to exercise that authority with consistency, setting reasonable standards, rules, and expectations—and sticking to them! Your child will respect you (and will welcome the guidance) if you present your expectations clearly, respectfully, and firmly in areas where you have real power to follow through with enforcement. You can say:

"What you do in your spare time is up to you, but I expect you to finish your homework and chores before you go out in the evening."

"I know that some of these subjects can be difficult and less enjoyable than others. Let's work on them together for a little while and see if we can clear up some of your confusion."

"If you think that expecting you to be home by 10 P.M. is unfair, then let's talk about it and see if we can reach a compromise. Does that sound fair enough to you?"

PITFALL #3: EXCESSIVE PRESSURE TO CONFORM

Parents of underachievers often attempt to mold their children in their own image rather than allowing them to grow as individuals. These domineering parents establish a battle of wills with their child by applying too much pressure to conform to unreasonable or preestablished goals. As a result, the child loses motivation and confidence because all he hears the parent saying is, *"What you are good at or want to do is not important or worthwhile. I know what's best for you."* Likewise, the parent becomes frustrated because the child does not respond to the pressure, sometimes rebelling outright.

A MORE EFFECTIVE APPROACH

Respecting your child's abilities and individuality can be balanced with guidance, reasonable standards, and exploring other options. For example, instead of saying, *"Artists starve, so you should be a lawyer,"* suggest going to the library together to research some of the careers related to art, such as advertising, architecture, graphic design, museum science, and so on. Then talk about what you have learned and discuss how these career options might fit into your child's abilities. You can say:

"Becoming an artist is a real challenge! What kinds of skills does one need to become an artist? What kinds of jobs and careers are available to artists? Let's go to the library and see what we can find out."

"I think you've got what it takes to become a professional artist. Which career in art do you think you would like to find out more about? Which career appeals to you the most? The least?"

"If being an artist is your goal and you are willing to put out the effort, then I'm behind you all the way! The important thing is that you strive to be as good an artist as you can and that you are happy with what you choose to do."

CONFIDENCE GROWS NATURALLY WHEN IT IS NURTURED

A sensitive balance between realistic praise, gentle criticism, and guidance is an effective way to build your child's self-esteem and confidence. Most children are resilient and fragile at the same time. One moment they want to be independent without restrictions, and the next minute they need to be told that they are loved, wanted, and respected. Whether your child is outgoing or shy, he or she still needs to hear you say, *"I am behind you all the way! You are a great kid and I love you!"*

GABBY GABOR'S
CONVERSATION CLINIC #8
ARE YOU A CONFIDENCE-BUSTER OR-BOOSTER?

The words you choose make a big difference to your child, but your attitude also comes through your voice and body language. Hurtful criticism, sarcasm, insensitive comments, unrealistic expectations, an overemphasis on competition, and the withholding of praise make a child feel lower than you can ever imagine. Every kid needs a pat on the back, so why not say, "Well done! I'm proud of you!"

Confidence-Buster

"How could you be so stupid?"

"If they can make the team, so can you."

Confidence-Booster

"We all make mistakes. Don't worry about it."

"Compete with yourself and don't worry about anyone else."

"You're hopeless! Anyone can do this. It's easy!"

"Be patient and take your time. It's hard, but you'll get it!"

"You want to be a professional ball player. That's ridiculous! You're nothing but a dreamer!"

"You've picked a tough goal, but if you work hard you have a chance of making it."

"This job isn't anywhere close to being right. This is awful!"

"You've got a good start so far. Now how can you improve it?"

"Why don't you be quiet and do it my way! I know better than you!"

"If we work on this job together we can get it done right."

"It doesn't matter what you think!"

"I'd like your feedback before I make a decision."

"You wouldn't understand, so why should I explain it to you?"

"I'd like to find out how you feel about the situation."

GETTING KIDS TO TALK ABOUT THEIR FEELINGS

Children learn from early on to hide their feelings because they are told by their parents, *"Grow up and act your age,"* or *"Big boys don't cry."* By the time youngsters reach the age of ten, they have learned all too well that revealing their true feelings can bring on ridicule, criticism, or punishment from their parents. When children are not encouraged to talk about their feelings as they enter and pass through adolescence, the communication channels with their parents can be, for all practical purposes, closed during this vital time.

"I can't talk now, I'm busy."

Many times kids want to talk to their parents about confusing issues or feelings that are troubling them, but they are given the implied message, *"Keep it to yourself."*

Instead of tuning into their child's feelings, some parents are too preoccupied with their own problems and assume that their kid's problem can wait, is unimportant, and will soon pass.

Furthermore, many parents feel unprepared to talk with their kids about difficult subjects such as sex, drugs, or divorce. They may believe that the less that is said about a taboo subject, the better. Denying a child the opportunity to express himself reinforces the inclination to hide feelings. As a result, he may suffer the consequences of coming to conclusions without the parent's feedback, clarification, or guidance. Once again the wrong message is sent to the child: *"Don't talk about your feelings."*

Discovering what is bothering a troubled youngster is difficult, especially if he or she hesitates to open up. Children often feel too guilty, ashamed, or embarrassed to talk about how they truly feel, and so they indirectly act out their feelings. There are also times when a child feels anxious or unhappy and may not even know why. It is at these times when communication between parent and child is most important.

OUTBURSTS USUALLY MEAN HIDDEN FEELINGS

Dear Gabby:

Most of the time my teenage daughter is cooperative and happy, but lately little things I say send her into a frenzy. For example, when I recently asked her to wash the dishes, she bellowed, "I'm sick of washing these stupid dishes!" *When I asked if there was some-*

thing wrong she cried out, "Nothing's wrong! Just leave me alone!" *What can I say to get her to open up?*

Signed,
Concerned Mother

When you ask your teenager to clear the dinner table and she flies into a screaming rage, chances are there is another issue that is affecting her behavior. Rather than yelling and calling her a lazy brat, encourage her to reveal whatever hidden feelings may have brought on the outburst. You can say something like,

"I didn't think my request was so unreasonable. Why are you getting so upset? What's the problem?"

"When people get upset over little things, there is usually something else going on. What is it?"

"Is there something bothering you that you would like to talk to me about?"

"I understand it is hard to talk about feelings, but I want you to know that I am willing to listen."

FREQUENT MOOD SWINGS MAY INDICATE A HIDDEN CONFLICT

"**I** *hate this place and everybody in it!"*

One day your kid is on cloud nine and the next day he acts like the world is going to end. While fluctuations in a child's behavior are normal, if you see a pattern of ups and downs in your child's mood, then look for hidden conflict. To encourage him to open up you can say,

"You seemed so happy yesterday and now you're down in the dumps. What gives?"

"If you are happier than a clam one day and down in the dumps the next, then something is bothering you. What is it?"

"You don't need to keep your feelings to yourself. If you tell me what's going on, maybe I can help, and besides, you will feel better if you talk about what's troubling you."

FIND THE REASON FOR A SUDDEN LACK OF INTEREST IN A FAVORITE ACTIVITY

"I don't want to go to band practice anymore—it's stupid!"

While it is natural for a child's enthusiasm to wax and wane, if he receives a harsh rejection, criticism, or rebuke related to a favorite activity, he may want to give it up entirely. Rather than ignore the comment and let your child's anger build out of proportion, use this opportunity to discuss the events that caused your youngster to lose interest. Chances are, if you openly talk about the situation, your child's perspective will improve and his enthusiasm for a favorite activity will return. You can say,

"You were so interested and involved in . . . and now you don't want to have anything to do with it. What happened to change your mind?"

To minimize the impact of a rejection or criticism on your youngster's self-esteem and confidence you can say,

"Even the best athletes (musicians, actors, dancers, etc.) get rejected or are criticized, but that does not prevent them from continuing to work hard at what they like to do and becoming successful."

"Rejections and criticism are part of life. You don't have to take them personally, but you can learn from them."

"Constructive criticism can help improve what you do."

"Remember the old proverb, 'If at first you don't succeed, then try again!' "

TALK OPENLY ABOUT DISCIPLINE OR LEARNING PROBLEMS

"**I** *don't want to go to school! I hate it! I hate my friends! I hate my teacher!"*

Divorce, a family illness, or any form of abuse are just a few of the factors that can impede a child's progress and create disciplinary problems in school. If you know some possible sources of your child's emotional conflict, inform his or her teachers. Without going into personal details, alert them that there are difficulties at home and ask them to contact you if they observe any adverse change in your child's schoolwork or classroom behavior. Then sit down with your child and honestly talk about the issues, even though they may be emotionally charged and hard to discuss. Share your feelings, too. To open the conversation you can say,

"I know that the situation at home is difficult and unpleasant. I feel bad about it, too. Let's talk about it so we can make the best of a hard situation."

"I want to talk about the trouble you've been having at school. What seems to be the problem?"

"How are you feeling about your mother and me getting a divorce (grandpa passing away, our new baby, etc.)? I know these feelings are hard to talk about, but instead of misbehaving in school, it is better to talk with me and honestly say you are angry, confused, and upset. I understand, because that's the way I feel, too."

ANTISOCIAL BEHAVIOR IS A SURE SIGN OF A TROUBLED CHILD

"**A**re you in trouble again?"

If serious emotional issues remain hidden, a child may misbehave in school, fight with classmates, or get into trouble because of sex, drugs, stealing, or vandalism. Your first reaction may be to punish the child, but upon closer examination of the circumstances leading up to his or her antisocial behavior, you may discover a pattern of misbehavior beginning with minor incidents, and then escalating to more serious confrontations with yourself, the school, or even the police.

CRYING OUT FOR ATTENTION

Children often seek attention when they feel upset, unloved, confused, abandoned, or left out of a situation, especially if the parents are preoccupied with demanding careers, a new child, personal problems, or financial difficulties. If your child seeks negative attention, then take the time to resolve some of the outstanding problems affecting his or her behavior. You can say,

"I know I have been very busy lately and haven't spent as much time with you as I would like, but I want to change that. How would you like to shoot some baskets (take a bike ride, walk on the beach, etc.) so we can talk and do something about the trouble you've been getting into lately."

"Let's face these problems together—head-on! When we work them out together we'll both be happier!"

If the parents and child make a commitment to spend more quality time together, honestly talk about feelings and expectations, plus agree on an acceptable behavior, then perhaps the child's attitude will improve. Keep in mind, however, that it usually takes more than just a few stern words to solve a serious behavior problem. Consider seeking professional counseling for you and your youngster, both separately and together. This will establish a concerted effort to discuss, alleviate, or at least minimize the causes of your child's behavior problems.

WHAT CAN A PARENT DO?

Talking about hidden feelings is a difficult task that requires sensitivity, patience, and above all, a trustful environment free of judgmental criticism. If you notice that your teenager is behaving in a peculiar way, take the initiative and say, *"Please, let's talk about what's bothering you."* Here are some other suggestions to improve your child's receptivity:

• Take an interest in your child's life from her perspective and show that you can listen and understand feelings above practicality.

• Encourage open and frank discussion of emotional topics.

• Tell your child that you accept and understand his or her feelings, and that there are ways to feeling happier.

TALKING ABOUT HIDDEN FEELINGS HELPS CHILDREN OVERCOME LIFE'S DIFFICULTIES

Most children go through difficult periods at one time or another. These are difficult times for parents as well, and working through them takes a commitment to face the issues with, and not against, your child. There are no easy answers, but one thing is for certain: when you line up on the same side as your kid, you are being understanding and supportive, and you are saying:

"I'm on your team and we are in this together."

GABBY GABOR'S
CONVERSATION CLINIC #9
TALKING TO A TROUBLED CHILD

A *child who has trouble in school or with the law needs special attention. Rather than threatening him with punishment, try a different approach. Explain that his behavior may indicate a deeper problem that needs to be faced head-on and that you are willing to work with him until you both find a solution. Keep in mind that most children test their parents', teachers', and society's limits. When kids learn that they cannot go beyond certain limits without consequences, their antisocial behavior often ends. To increase your child's receptivity to working with you, you can say:*

"How do you feel about how things are going for you?"

"What do you want that you are not getting now?"

"In what ways would you like your life to be different?"

"How do you think your attitude affects how others treat you?"

"If you could do anything you wanted, what would it be?"

"What specific things could you do to make the changes you want?"

"If you are not responsible for your actions, then who is?"

"You can make your life what you want it to be. It's up to you. You are in control if you are willing to take the responsibility."

"You've got a lot of things going for you, so why not give yourself a chance to do something satisfying with your life?"

"Facing problems is something everyone has to do, but it's not so scary if you are willing to share them with someone you trust."

"We both know that your attitude could improve. Is there any way that you are willing to change it?"

"Are you willing to work together to straighten out some of your problems? Are there any specific ways that I can be of help?"

chapter 10

TALKING TO YOUR CHILD ABOUT SEX, DRUGS, AND DIVORCE

There is no question that many parents feel uncomfortable about or even incapable of talking to their children about sex, drugs, or divorce. In the past, the "facts of life" were often the most sensitive topic that parents discussed with their children, but today AIDS, drug and alcohol abuse, and divorce lead the list. If you have put off talking about these touchy subjects with your child, then now is the time to start.

Dear Gabby:

My ten-year-old son is asking me questions about sex and I'm not sure what to tell him. Is he too young to

*learn about reproduction, birth control, and the threat
of AIDS, or should I let him find out on his own?
What should I tell him?*

Signed,
Embarrassed Parent

PARENTS FEAR TALKING ABOUT SEX MORE THAN THEIR KIDS DO

Sex—what could be more fascinating and confusing to
a child? It is perfectly natural for children as young as
three years old to be curious about sex and ask questions
like, *"Where do babies come from?"* As children become
adolescents, their interest in sex intensifies because this
is a time of sexual growth, experimentation, and striving
for independence.

Many parents assume, or hope, that their kids will
learn about sex in school, at church, or from friends,
and as a result avoid the discussion altogether or hastily
dismiss the subject with a cursory, *"You know the birds
and the bees don't you?"* However, most family counselors suggest that the earlier sex education begins in the
home, the easier it is for parents and the more beneficial
it is for the child.

GOOD SEX EDUCATION = FACTUAL INFORMATION + FAMILY VALUES

Before sitting down to discuss sex and related topics,
you may wish to visit your local library to find answers
to any questions you may have or call your child's school
and request information about sex-education classes

being offered. Review the materials, ask questions, and talk to teachers, your clergy, your family doctor, or health-care professionals. Having questions about sex is not a crime, but avoiding honest answers can be deadly!

Most parents attempt to pass their sexual values down to their children, and do so with varying degrees of success. Saying, *"If you get pregnant (or get someone else pregnant), don't bother coming home,"* however, will only alienate your child, making her afraid to talk about or ask questions related to sex. Experts agree that open and frank discussions with your son or daughter to communicate accurate information, family values, and expectations, are much more effective than attempting to dictate sexual behavior.

When you are ready, sit down with your child and go over the materials together. Do not worry that you are putting the idea of sex into your child's head because it is already there, thanks to television, movies, advertising—and natural curiosity! In addition, parents who received their sex education on their own often discover answers to longtime questions, or clear up misconceptions, when they learn about sex along with their children. For a young child you might open the conversation with,

"Have you ever wondered where babies come from? Here is a book I want to read with you that explains how men and women make love and how they make a baby."

"You don't have to feel embarrassed to talk about sex. I'll try to answer any questions you have, and if I don't know the answers, then we'll find out the answers together by looking them up or asking someone like our family doctor."

If your child asks you an explicit question such as *"Do you and Daddy do* it?" you can say,

"If you mean intercourse, yes. That is one way we show our love for each other."

"Yes, because that's one way men and women show their love for each other."

"Yes, because we want to have another baby."

If your child asks you an explicit question that is inappropriate, poorly timed, or one that you would just rather not answer, you can say,

"That is a private matter between your mother and myself."

"That is something we can talk about when you are a little older."

"Now is not the right time to talk about that subject. We can discuss it later."

To encourage an open dialogue with teenagers about sexually related topics, you can say,

"Learning the right information and attitude about sex and love is important. Understanding sex is more than just knowing 'the facts of life.' "

"Let's talk about sexual responsibility."

"Let's talk about teen pregnancy."

"Let's talk about birth control."

"What are your feelings about abortion?"

"What facts do you know about AIDS?"

Experts suggest these additional do's and don'ts when discussing sexual issues with your child:

D o answer your child's questions about sex as honestly and completely as you can.

D o n ' t be embarrassed to say, *"I don't know, let's find out."*

D o take into account your child's age when you answer questions about sex.

D o n ' t use slang when answering your child's questions about sexual organs, bodily functions, or reproduction.

D o start your child's sex education early with accurate information and positive family values.

D o n ' t go into long explanations to answer your child's questions about sex.

D o be direct and specific.

D o n ' t expect one session of questions and answers to end your youngster's curiosity about sex.

D o be prepared to explain and answer the same questions frequently, giving more details as your child's understanding and experience increases. The more frequently you talk about sex, the easier and more comfortable it will be to discuss.

ALCOHOL, DRUG ABUSE, AND CIGARETTES

Dear Gabby:

My teenager says everyone in his school smokes, drinks, and uses drugs. Do you think that encouraging him to "Just say no!" is enough to keep him from participating? What else can I say?

Signed,
Frightened Parent

Like it or not, cigarettes, alcohol, and drugs are part of our world and youngsters do experiment with them.

Keep in mind, however, that there is a difference between normal curiosity, which leads to experimentation, and substance abuse. A parent's best line of defense against his child falling prey to alcohol or drug abuse is to set a good example at home, have open communication about personal problems, and learn about addiction through education. You and your child may want to attend drug and alcohol education programs that are available in schools, libraries, churches, or community centers. Then discuss what you have learned without cross-examining or demanding a confession from your youngster. You can encourage open discussion by asking questions such as,

"What do you think about the drug-abuse issue?"

"Why do you think some kids feel that drugs, cigarettes, or alcohol make them more popular with their friends?"

"What ways do you think television, movies, and advertising affect how people deal with alcohol, cigarettes, and drugs?"

"How does it feel to be pressured by friends to use drugs or alcohol? How can you deal with peer pressure to use drugs, cigarettes, or alcohol?"

"How do you think drugs, cigarettes, and alcohol affect a person's body, people at work, pregnant mothers, young children, and kids trying to learn in school?"

"Do you know anyone who has a problem with drugs or alcohol?"

"What do you think can be done to help solve the problem?"

KIDS ARE OFTEN BETTER INFORMED THAN THEIR PARENTS

Due to increased drug-education programs in school, many children are better informed about substance abuse than their parents, so it is worthwhile to do some research of your own on the topic. When you have discussions with your child about substance abuse, be prepared for answers or information that you may find upsetting. However, it is better to talk honestly about drugs than to pretend that the problem does not exist or that your child is immune. Remain calm and under no circumstances punish your child for being candid and open with you. In this particular situation it may be better to say less and listen more, thus establishing a communication bridge between you and your child. To show your child that you appreciate his honesty you can say,

"What you have told me is very upsetting, but I'm glad you are being honest with me."

"I want you to know that I've learned a lot about this problem from talking with you and I think I understand it better now. Let's talk again soon."

DIVORCE AND STEPFAMILY RELATIONSHIPS

Dear Gabby:

After ten years of an unhappy marriage, my wife and I have decided to get a divorce, but we don't know how to tell our eight-year-old son about our decision. Should we put it off as long as possible, make up a story, or tell him the hard truth now?

Signed,
Guilty Father

Divorce is one of the most stressful experiences children and parents face. What can you say to your child to make him feel better or more secure at this difficult time? There are no easy answers, but how parents explain and cope with this unhappy situation does make a difference to their child's well-being. Experts suggest that open, honest, and sensitive communication can help parents and children through the painful process of divorce. They point out that once the decision is made to divorce, it is best for both parents to sit down together with their child to calmly explain how their family situation is going to change.

HOW TO TELL YOUR CHILD YOU ARE GETTING A DIVORCE

Parents say that informing their child of a pending divorce is one of the most unhappy moments they face. Even after years of hearing parents argue, it is common that the first time a child hears about divorce is after one parent has already left. Instead of making excuses, lying, or making false promises, experts suggest saying something like,

"Your mother and I were once in love, but we have not been happy together for a long time. It's difficult to explain, but we have tried to work things out, and couldn't. So, after a lot of careful thinking we have decided that it is best that your mother and I get divorced. This means that she and I will stop being married to each other and will not live together anymore."

"We want you to understand that husbands and wives get divorced from each other, but not from their children. We will always be your parents and love you very much."

"We both still love you very much and that is never going to change. We will always be your mother and father, even though you will not live with both of us at the same time."

"We know this is very upsetting, that you are probably angry, and that you do not want this to happen, but it is best for everyone. We want you to know that you are not to blame. No one is to blame."

"We know that you will have a lot of questions and we will try to answer them as well as we can."

"We want you to know that there are going to be some changes in our family. You are going to live here with me some of the time and with your mother some of the time."

"Divorce is not a happy time for any of us but it is a fact that everyone in our family must learn to live with. Even though we are sad now, we will get through it and our lives will go on."

THE STEPFAMILY RELATIONSHIP: BUILDING COMMUNICATION BRIDGES BETWEEN TWO FAMILIES

Dear Gabby:

After being divorced for three years, I'm planning to remarry soon. Will combining two families cause any particular communication problems?

Signed,
Soon-to-Be-Stepparent

Contrary to popular belief, the majority of stepfamilies do not "blend" into one reconstructed family. On

the contrary, individual families of a step relationship remain separate from one another, and expecting them to merge into a "dream family" is just one of several unrealistic expectations that can hinder a new stepfamily's chances of success. To avoid this pitfall, openly discuss issues and styles that make your two families similar or different. For example you can say,

"In our family we like to . . . What does your family like?"

"It has always been a rule in our family to . . . What are your family rules?"

"It seems natural that our two families may do things differently. That doesn't mean that one family is right and the other is wrong—it just means they do things differently."

"Sometimes different family styles can cause problems or hurt someone's feelings. I think we all need to be careful and be a little extra sensitive to the other person's feelings. What do you think about that? How do you think we can do that?"

STEPFAMILY MEMBERS DO NOT INSTANTLY LOVE EACH OTHER

A stepparent anxious to please her new spouse may try extra hard to love his children as if they were her own, only to find her overtures rejected. Expecting instant love is unrealistic and can scuttle the step relationship right from the beginning, leaving everyone disappointed, bitter, and withdrawn. To avoid this potential problem you can say,

"It is okay not to love a new stepparent or stepchild right away, because love between stepfamily members requires a lot of time and trust to develop."

"It is not necessary to love your new stepparent, stepsister, or stepbrother, but politeness and mutual respect are essential."

THE STEPPARENT DOES NOT REPLACE THE BIOLOGICAL PARENT

Many new stepparents soon discover that their stepchild's "blood is thicker than water" and that a child's absent biological parent is often viewed as a saint. Even if the biological father is negligent, a stepchild will often feel that he can do no wrong. Attempting to usurp the biological parent's position usually creates more confusion for the child, and resentment toward the stepparent. To let your stepchild know that you understand your special relationship, you can say,

"Even though I'm married to your mother now, I understand that I'm not going to replace your father. I just hope that we can become really good friends!"

"I'm your stepmother and I don't expect you to love me like you love your mother, and that's okay. Our feelings for one another will be different."

"You are my stepchild and I love you, but your mother and father will always be your parents even though they don't still live together."

DISCIPLINE IS THE JOB OF THE BIOLOGICAL PARENT AND THE STEPPARENT

New stepparents are often confused about discipline in the step relationship. Many believe that they can avoid the stigma of the "mean stepmother" by leaving all the disciplining to the biological parents. While it is better for the biological parent to punish a misbehaving child, the stepparent also has an important role to play. To avoid an inconsistent set of rules that are enforced by the biological parent but not the stepparent, tell your children in a firm, but pleasant voice,

"Your stepfather and I have explained the house rules to you and we expect that you will follow them as best you can."

"Your stepmother and I expect you to be respectful and polite."

If you are a stepparent and your stepchild responds that in his other house he does not have to be polite, follow rules, do chores, and so on, you can say,

"That may be, but in this house all of us are courteous, help around the house, answer each other, and use good manners."

"I may not be your mother (or father) but I still expect you to follow the rules and do your part around this house. That's not too much to ask—is it?"

TALKING TO KIDS ABOUT DIFFICULT ISSUES PAYS OFF

It is not easy to talk to kids about personal subjects or topics which you both feel strongly about. In all probability, your child already has established opinions, very probably in conflict with yours. After all, how many parents and kids, especially teenagers, see eye-to-eye on sex, drugs, or other controversial issues?

Even so, smart parents can avoid constant conflict with their child if they keep in mind that communicating is not simply for the purpose of imposing their will. Open communication about sensitive subjects establishes an environment that is conducive to frank conversation about any topic. This means that when a parent presents his or her viewpoint, the child has the opportunity to do the same. That way a parent can exert considerable influence, while at the same time respecting his or her child's opinions and right to speak.

GABBY GABOR'S CONVERSATION CLINIC #10

STRATEGIES FOR SAYING "NO THANKS" TO ALCOHOL

Tell your teenager that you understand that alcohol is part of socializing, and that it can be difficult to decline a drink, but that it is often necessary, especially if he or she is driving. Explain that it takes skill to learn how to drink, and that moderation, self-control, and responsibility are essential to avoid problems with alcohol. Point out that the drinking habits established in early adulthood often stick with a person throughout his or her life. The following strategies are designed to encourage a teenager to make intelligent choices when faced with peer pressure to drink. You can say,

---

"There is always peer pressure to drink, whether you are a teenager or an adult. People will offer you a drink to be polite, but it is your decision to accept or reject it. Don't let others make the choice for you. If you do not want an alcoholic

beverage, simply say in a firm but friendly voice, 'No thanks, I'd prefer a soft drink.' "

"Your friends may pressure you to drink. If you decide not to, then firmly say, 'No thanks.' If they tease you or persist by asking you why not, then say, 'I don't feel like it, period.' Abstaining in this situation is easier if you say, 'I'll be the nondrinking driver tonight.' If your friends do not respect your decision, then maybe they are not such good friends."

"If you do decide to accept a drink, keep in mind that drinking alcohol requires skill. Make a drink last longer by sipping it slowly, and always eat something at the same time. Never drink on an empty stomach."

"Never try to impress anyone with how much alcohol you can drink, and always put a limit on your number of drinks. Once you reach your limit, even if it is just one or two drinks, then stop and ask for a soft drink or club soda with a cherry or lemon twist."

"If you feel dizzy, immediately stop drinking, get some fresh air, wash your face, and have something light to eat. Never operate a car if you feel dizzy, or be a passenger with a driver who has been drinking. Even one alcoholic drink can slow a driver's reaction time enough to make the difference between life and death."

"It doesn't matter what time it is—I want you to call me (or a cab) to come pick you up if you cannot get home in a car driven by a nondrinking driver. And don't worry, you won't be punished for calling."

IMPROVING

YOUR FAMILY'S

CONVERSATION

NETWORK

When it comes to family conversations, you have a choice. Open communication . . .

"Everyone in my family has an opinion—right or wrong. Sometimes you argue and sometimes you agree, but you always have a chance to speak your mind."

Or closed communication . . .

"My father made all the decisions in our family. If someone disagreed or tried to present a different opinion we usually ended up in a fight. I think everyone finally just gave up!"

THE CONVERSATION NETWORK IS THE FAMILY'S LIFELINE

Everyone knows that love and affection are vital for a happy family. However, family counselors and other mental-health professionals agree that frequent and meaningful communication between all family members is crucial for resolving issues, heading off destructive confrontations, and reinforcing family unity. Without open conversation, a family's growth can be stunted by resentment, conflict, and passivity.

While all families are unique, most cope with the same basic issues, such as maintaining a secure home, dealing with daily responsibilities, caring for each other's physical and emotional needs, and adapting to new situations. How can a family protect itself from the many obstacles it faces, yet remain flexible enough to adjust to constant change?

The answer to this question lies in the family's ability to establish a conversation network that provides an equal opportunity for airing grievances, presenting opposing viewpoints and, most important, creating mutual respect for all its members regardless of their position in the family. Once the network is functioning, parents and children alike will understand where other members stand on vital issues that affect their family. In this way, the conversation network is the family's lifeline. If one member feels troubled, has difficulty coping, or seeks someone to confide in, the family's unity provides personal strength and emotional support.

BUILDING YOUR FAMILY'S CONVERSATION NETWORK

An effective conversation network can be built in a relatively short time, but requires both consistency and flexibility to continue growing. The network is based on parents following these principles:

1. First talk with your spouse about household rules, expectations, and discipline—then present the policy as co-leaders of your household.

Parents must be co-leaders of their family if there is to be consistency and fairness in the home. If there is no couple unity, how can there be family unity? Unified family leadership is based on compromises and agreements by the parents and then presented to the children as one policy. When parents agree on and establish a basic framework of rules, expectations, and discipline upon which they and other family members can rely and build, then their family unit will be more cohesive.

If you and your spouse disagree on a matter of family discipline, suggest discussing the issue at another time soon, sticking to the rules you have already agreed upon. When discussing family policy with your spouse you can say,

"Let's first decide between the two of us what house rules we want to discuss with the kids. That way they'll know that we mean business, we will not be played off one against the other, and the rules will be consistent."

When discussing family policy with your kids, be friendly but firm by saying something like,

"We have clearly defined rules in our house and we expect them to be followed as best you can."

"If you disagree with our rules, let's talk about them now and come to an agreement that we can all live with."

2. Mealtimes and other family rituals provide important opportunities for conversation.

Today's families have a limited amount of time to spend together, so household rituals such as evening meals, leisure activities, weekend breakfasts, and group projects are more important than ever. These times together provide members with an opportunity to exchange news, make plans, reveal feelings, discuss family issues, air pet peeves, and have fun. It is during these ritual meetings that parents and children can discuss rules, expectations, share experiences, and talk about other issues which affect the entire family. To alert your child that you want to bring up a particular topic during dinner, for example, you can say,

"I've planned your favorite meal for tomorrow night and your father and I want to start making plans for our family vacation. We want to know what you would like to do this summer, so think about it and we'll discuss it over dinner."

3. Each member contributes to the family's daily operation.

When all members contribute to the overall household family operation, then everyone in the family benefits. It is for this reason that the assigning and completion of specific family jobs is a crucial factor. The question is, who does what jobs, and what rewards or consequences await those who comply and those who cop out? Deciding who does what task is one area where family decision-making can really pay off. By rotating chores, no one member will feel stuck with an undesirable job while an older brother or sister gets off easy simply because of his or her position in the family hierarchy. One fun way to assign household tasks is to hold a "chore auction." You can say,

"The following chores are up for bid—first come, first served! Who wants to mow the lawn in return for...? Weed the garden in return for...? Wash the car in return for...?

EXPAND YOUR FAMILY'S CONVERSATION NETWORK EVERY DAY

When warmth and affection are expressed apart from specific behavior, and not provided as a reward or withheld as punishment, family members will know they are loved and wanted. Above all, the ability to converse openly with family members about your feelings, fears, dreams, goals, hopes, and needs will establish a firm footing upon which your family can grow and adapt to a swiftly changing world.

A family network is dependent upon consistent, respectful two-way communication. Topics such as meals, chores, or weekend activities are usually easier to discuss than the more volatile issues of divorce, sex, or stepparents. However, if you practice your conversation skills on these everyday topics, talking about emotional issues is easier because communication skills such as listening, good body language, asking information-seeking questions, and self-disclosure are already well established. In the end, it is not so much what you say, but the fact that you are communicating on a daily basis that makes your conversation network an effective tool for building and maintaining your family's happiness.

GABBY GABOR'S
CONVERSATION CLINIC #11
MAKING A FAMILY DECISION

When family members get together on a regular basis to discuss important issues and make decisions, everyone benefits. The key to family decision-making is to give everyone the opportunity to express his or her opinion, encourage discussion, and try to find solutions based on compromise. Here are some other tips:

1. Announce the topic of discussion a few days ahead of time. A note on the refrigerator will do. For example, it can say, *"Family Meeting: Tuesday evening, after dinner. Topic: Should we adopt a pet from the humane society?"*

2. Remind family members that everyone has the right to express his or her opinion without interruption. You can say, *"If you don't agree with what someone says, just wait your turn. Everyone will get a chance to speak."*

3. Open the topic for discussion by saying, *"Do we really want to adopt a pet? Billy, it's your idea, so let's hear from you first."*

4. Encourage discussion of all sides of an issue by saying, *"It's true that there are a lot of animals that need homes, but taking care of a pet is a big responsibility and costs extra money too. Who has some other thoughts on this subject?"*

5. **Ask family members to seek creative solutions or compromises to unresolved issues.** You can say, *"Let's take a few minutes to brainstorm together and see if we can come up with an answer to the questions we have raised tonight."*

6. **Summarize all suggestions and viewpoints** by saying, *"Billy wants to adopt a dog and start a dog-walking business to pay for the cost of pet food. Meg wants to adopt a kitten because cats are easier to take care of than dogs, and Jena wants to adopt a dog and a cat so they will have company. Your father and I don't mind adopting a pet as long as we won't have to nag you to do your other chores."*

7. **Remind the kids that you have the final say,** and complete the family discussion by saying, *"I'm glad we talked this idea over together before your father and I make a decision."*

ASSERTIVE CONVERSATIONS WITH YOUR PARENTS

BREAKING OLD PATTERNS THAT CAUSE CONFLICT

Dear Gabby:

I love my parents dearly, but they always criticize and tell me what to do. True, I'm not always as mature as I could be, but I am grown up now with a family

of my own! How can I tell them to treat me more like
an adult wihout causing a big blowup?

Signed,
Grown Child

Most children do not see their parents as real people
grappling with life's challenges, but rather as all-
powerful beings with answers for everything. A child's
view of his parents is usually one of provider, protector,
helper, and authority. This view gradually changes as
the child enters adolescence and learns that his parents
are fallible and do not always make the right choices.
At the same time, when parents see their child can make
responsible decisions, they can shed their superparent
status. However, if both the adult child and parents continue to operate under the old patterns that governed
childhood and adolescence, then there may be conflict.

UNFULFILLED EXPECTATIONS + WITHHELD APPROVAL = CONFLICT

"**Y**ou should be making more money. You should be
doing more with your life. When I was your age I was
married and had two kids! When are you going to grow
up?"

Most children receive approval by meeting their parents' expectations but many are denied praise if they
fail or choose alternative goals. However, as an adult,

one must balance a desire for independence with the
need for parental approval. As a result, conflict between
a parent and adult child may flare up over these issues:

Marital status   *Friends*

Child-rearing practices   *Lifestyles*

Financial responsibilities   *Frequency of visits*

Personal goals   *Personal habits*

Priorities   *Family communication*

Borrowed money   *Substance abuse*

CHANGING OLD PATTERNS IS NOT EASY, BUT IT CAN BE DONE

Old family patterns are hard to break for both parents
and their adult children. Many parents consider giving
advice to their grown children, whether it is solicited
or not, as part of their responsibility, and feel hurt or
get angry if their suggestions are rejected or ignored.
On the other hand, grown children resent their parents
treating them as if they are still children without experience, common sense, or capabilities of their own.
So what is the answer to this dilemma?

ASSERTIVE CONVERSATIONS IMPROVE PARENT AND ADULT CHILD COMMUNICATION

Conflicts between parents and their adult children can
be minimized if both learn how to assertively communicate with each other. If parents avoid manipulative

comments and adult children become less sensitive to parental criticism, there will be a decline in the defensive behavior that sets off arguments. The following three examples are typical problem areas where assertive conversations can improve parent and adult-child communication.

EXAMPLE #1: DEALING WITH A DOMINEERING PARENT

Parent's manipulative comment: *"You are still my baby, and I know what's best for you."*

Adult child's unassertive response: *"Quit treating me like a little girl!"*

Parents must eventually let go and allow their grown child to make her own decisions, live with her mistakes, and lead her own life. They can show that they have confidence in their adult child's judgment by acknowledging her ability to make decisions.

The adult child can remove the automatic response of the domineering parent by apologizing for immature behavior while asserting the right to make personal choices, even if they conflict with her parent's wishes or goals. To acknowledge a past indiscretion you can say, *"I realize that sometimes I do or say things that are thoughtless. I apologize."*

Parent's assertive comment: *"It's your decision. I'm sure you know what you're doing."*

The adult-child can then follow up with:

"I appreciate you thinking about me, but I've got to decide what is best for me."

"I understand that you are concerned about my future. Let me explain how I see the situation."

"I want you to know how I made my final decision."

EXAMPLE # 2 : DEALING WITH PARENTAL ADVICE

Parent's manipulative comment: *"Let me tell you how you should do it. I'm a little older and a lot wiser!"*

Adult child's unassertive response: *"Don't tell me what to do! I'm not a baby, you know!"*

Adult children can demonstrate to their parents that they are mature, independent, and capable by showing a willingness to listen to advice (and even to ask for it before it is given), but in the end taking responsibility for their own actions and decisions.

Adult child's assertive comment: *"You have come up with some interesting ideas. I'll think about what you have said."*

"I think many of the points you brought up make good sense. Thanks for the advice."

"Your suggestions will help me make an intelligent decision."

By the same token, if parents offer their advice without suggesting that their adult child is incapable of managing on his own, then their input may be welcome.

Parent's assertive comment: *"I'm sure you've got the situation under control, but if you're interested, I've got a few ideas that you might find helpful."*

"Do you want my advice for what it is worth? You're free to take it or leave it. You know what's best for you."

EXAMPLE #3: DEALING WITH PARENTAL CRITICISM

Parent's manipulative comment: *"You've got to be out of your mind to spend money on a car like that!"*

Adult child's unassertive response: *"Why do you think that you know everything?"*

Parents create needless conflict by criticizing their adult child's choices, often from habit. But when a grown child feels confident about his own decisions, so that praise from a parent is welcome, but not necessary—or when he recognizes that parental criticism is an old pattern—he can become less sensitive and defensive about it. He can respnod to such criticism by saying assertively,

"I know that you probably would not choose this kind of car, but my needs are different and this is what I have been saving for."

"I respect your right to disagree with me, but it is my decision."

"I'd like to have your support, but if I don't that's okay too."

Similarly, parents can avoid conflict with their adult child by replacing criticism with praise or enthusiasm even if their choices differ.

Parent's assertive comment: *"I'm sure you have shopped around for the best deal you could find. You sure picked out a beautiful automobile!"*

THE GOAL IS AN ADULT-TO-ADULT COMMUNICATION

An adult relationship is based on equality and mutual respect. For the adult child, it is respect for one's parents, their experience, insight, and the knowledge they have to offer. And in turn, for the parent, it is accepting the right of one's grown child to make his or her own decisions, formulate goals, determine priorities, or march to the beat of a different drummer.

CHANGING PATTERNS TAKES TIME

It takes many assertive conversations for parents and their adult children to alter patterns which have developed over a lifetime. These adjustments do not occur overnight, but take place gradually. When parents and adult children assertively communicate with each other, their relationship is bound to improve, and with it their mutual happiness and well-being.

Here are some additional conversation do's and don'ts when talking with senior citizens:

D o show an interest in their opinions, feelings, and observations. You can say, *"How have you seen things change over the years?"* or *"How do you feel about . . . ?"*

D o n ' t be patronizing. Don't say, *"You probably wouldn't understand;"* or *"Isn't that nice."*

D o ask questions about current events, movies, books, music, hobbies, or other topics of interest. You can say, *"What good books or articles have you read lately?"* or *"How is your chess game these days?"*

D o n ' t interrupt or put words into a senior's mouth. Don't say, *"Yeah, but . . ."* or *"Let me explain what you mean."*

D o allow more time for seniors to formulate thoughts and sentences. You can say, *"Take your time, I'm listening."*

D o n ' t assume that a senior citizen cannot deal with a tough situation. Don't say, *"You can't handle this. I'll do the talking."*

D o encourage seniors to reminisce. You can say, *"I'd love to hear about where you grew up, your work before you retired, or a special time or person in your life."*

D o n ' t shout because you assume that all senior citizens are hard of hearing. Speak in a normal tone of voice, but face him or her so your mouth is visible.

D o share some of your feelings, opinions, and goals in areas where you may have common interests. You can say, *"Like you, I am interested in . . ."*

GABBY GABOR'S
CONVERSATION CLINIC #12
TIPS FOR HAPPIER VISITS WITH PARENTS

Visiting with parents can be stressful under the best circumstances. Start with a positive attitude by saying, "I'm here to have fun and visit with the people I love. I've been looking forward to this visit for quite a while and I know we are going to have a great time!" *Be aware that emotions are highest at the beginning and end of visits, so avoid overreaction to comments or questions that may seem confrontational. Accept your folks for their good points and keep in mind that they are people too and not just your parents.*

---

1. Establish a set of behavior ground rules to avoid old arguments. For example, you can say, *"I don't want to argue over little things, so I promise to be home early most nights (not be late for dinner, help around the house, etc.) if you promise not to bug me too much about what I wear (who I see, how I fix my hair, etc.)."*

2. Desensitize yourself to old disputes that set off arguments, and make an extra effort to show your parents that you are a mature and responsible adult. Nip tensions in the bud by saying, *"Let's get along and enjoy the short time we have to spend together."*

3. If your past visits have started off peacefully but after a time end up in old arguments, then plan for a shorter stay. If your parents protest, say, *"The quality of our visit is more important than how long we visit, especially if we end up arguing."*

4. Avoid criticizing your parents, even if they criticize you. Chances are, their opinions and values are not going to change. Your best response to parental criticism is, *"I understand you do not approve of my lifestyle, but I'm the one who must decide what is best for me."*

5. Spend plenty of time talking with your parents about the important, rewarding, and exciting things happening in their life as well as yours. You can say, *"So enough about me. How are your plans coming along for your dream vacation?"*

6. Limit your discussion of personal problems or complaints. You are visiting to share time with your parents. Don't expect them to solve your problems. Say, *"Don't worry, I can handle these problems on my own."*

7. Let your parents know that you are planning to spend time with friends as well. Set aside some free time to visit friends or go away for a day or two. Say, *"I'm also planning on spending some time with my friend Jody. We haven't seen each other for years and want to catch up on old times."*

8. Always be a gracious guest and offer assistance with the dishes or dinner, help around the house, or find other ways to show your appreciation. Always send a short note soon after your visit is over, saying, *"Thanks, I had a wonderful time!"*

DEFUSING

A FAMILY

FEUD

"*At the time I was so angry with my uncle I could have screamed, but it's been so long since we've talked, that I can barely remember what we were arguing about.*"

A family feud is one of the most destructive forces that can be thrust upon a household, and the causes are often as clouded as the solutions. Maybe it started because of an irresponsible comment, a broken promise, competition between a spouse and an in-law, conflicting priorities, incompatible personalities, alcoholism, drug addiction, or an unfair accusation that left a relative's feelings in shambles.

While there are clear-cut reasons for some family feuds, if the fighting seems to be over petty differences, then there may be a hidden source of conflict. If the real reasons for a family feud are dealt with early on, then the damage can be minimized. If, however, the feuding is allowed to grow unabated, then the family's very existence is threatened.

THE HIGH PRICE OF A FAMILY FEUD

Whatever the reasons for personal feuds, if relatives constantly argue or stop talking to each other altogether, everyone in the family suffers. Who is right and who is wrong pales compared to the damage an estrangement can inflict on the family's emotional health. In most cases, the ruinous effects of a family feud far outweigh the causes that spawned the conflict in the first place. The ties that bind the family together are stretched, leaving its members feeling bitter, resentful, and cheated.

A TIME FOR RECONCILIATION

Once relatives recognize that the emotional costs of a family feud far outweigh the original causes, then it is time for reconciliation. Although the people directly at odds may feel uncomfortable at the thought of getting together, the payoff for the entire family is worth the effort. In some cases, a grave illness or death of a close relative creates the impetus for family members to bury the hatchet. Whatever the reasons, when relatives stop feuding, everyone in the family benefits.

HOLDING OUT AN OLIVE BRANCH

The desirability of restoring good family relations may not be as obvious as the arguments that caused the feud. In many cases, there is no specific peace settlement, but rather a friendly gesture such as a birthday card, a note of congratulations, or a willingness of one person to help the other in some way. So if you see any signals that indicate a willingness to let bygones be bygones, take the initiative to start the healing process. If one of the feuding parties holds out an olive branch, but the other party ignores or misses the signal, the chance for a settlement may not return for a long time to come.

DEFUSING THE CONFLICT

Sometimes there are matters which need to be resolved before feuding family members can become friends again. If this is the case, consider the following strategies:

- If you do not want to approach your relative in person, present your peace proposal in a letter, phone call, or through a neutral third party. People often respond more openly and less defensively to overtures presented in letters or over the phone than they do in a face-to-face confrontation. You can say, *"I know we have had our differences about . . . , but I would like to find a compromise and work them out for our family's sake. I want to make up and be friends again."*

- Clearly summarize your points, but avoid accusatory statements such as, *"You always do this!"* or

"You're acting just like your father (brother, sister, etc.)."

• When you reveal your feelings choose words that heal the wounds instead of tearing them more. You can say, *"I value our family's happiness more than proving a point of who is right or wrong. Let's end this feud once and for all."*

• Even if you feel that your relative is acting immaturely, make it a point to show your willingness to admit past mistakes, forgive and forget. You can say, *"Come on, we all make mistakes and I apologize for mine. I don't think that this is worth arguing over anymore."*

• Limit your disagreement. You can say, *"I don't want our differences of opinion to destroy our family. How about if we just agree to disagree and leave it at that?"*

• Since feuds can often be traced to hurt feelings rather than to a specific disagreement, a sincere apology can go a long way to repair the emotional damage. You can say, *"I just want you to know that I'm sorry for what I said and for hurting your feelings. I apologize and I hope you can forgive me."*

• Take responsibility for your role in the dispute. You can say, *"I hate it when we fight like this and what it does to the rest of the family. I know that I fly off the handle sometimes, but I've promised myself to be less critical when we are together."*

• Suggest reasons not to be angry. When you come to the conclusion that the original argument is no longer important you can say, *"Enough is enough. I'm not angry anymore and for the sake of the family, what do you say we bury the hatchet?"*

- A sincere show of affection can defuse an argument before it escalates into a full-blown feud. Try giving your relative a warm hug and say, *"I love you even if we don't always agree."*

- Consider talking to a clergyman, health-care professional, or family counselor as a method of mediating a compromise solution. You can say, *"This fighting is tearing our family apart and we can't seem to resolve it ourselves. How do you feel about talking to someone who might help us find a solution to this problem once and for all?"*

NOT ALL FAMILY CONFLICTS CAN BE RESOLVED

Sometimes an angry person may not respond to overtures and agree to end the feud, because some violations are unforgivable and no amount of negotiating or apologies will rectify the situation. In these instances, take a civil attitude by attempting to patch up the relationship on the surface. While this approach will not resolve the underlying conflict, it may allow the family to function more normally. If your family's happiness is the goal, instead of winning the argument or even resolving the conflict, then compromising to the point of talking without animosity is an acceptable alternative for the present. In time, there may be a possibility of renewing the friendship too.

THE SOONER YOU REUNITE THE BETTER IT IS FOR YOUR FAMILY

You do not have to wait for a relative's close brush with death to end a feud. However, in many cases, even if two stubborn people want to end a long-standing quarrel, they will wait because neither one is willing to make the first move. When someone sooner or later takes the initiative to break the ice and reestablish contact, the entire family will benefit, and in some cases the onetime enemies can eventualy become good friends, claiming that their friendship grew by resolving a difficult problem between them. When this happens, relatives can feel thankful for the time they get to spend together as friends. Plus your family can recover from the emotional damage, regain its stability, and grow closer in the years to come.

GABBY GABOR'S CONVERSATION CLINIC #13
DEALING WITH PROBLEM IN-LAWS

Your in-laws! They can be the bane of your existence or fill your life with joy, support, and love. In either case, they are a force to be reckoned with, because how you communicate with your in-laws makes all the difference in the world to your spouse and his or her family. To improve communication with your in-laws keep the following points in mind:

1. Rather than confront your in-laws on every difference of opinion, be willing to compromise on issues that are important to them. This shows that you are flexible. You can say, *"If it makes you happy, I'm willing to . . ."*

2. Be assertive about issues that you feel strongly about and that affect you and your spouse directly, such as where you live, or child-rearing practices. You can say, *"I understand how you feel about it, and we appreciate your suggestions, but we have discussed it and decided together that it is best for us if we . . ."*

3. Avoid a "no-win situation" such as playing mediator, defender, or prosecutor if your in-laws and spouse argue. If you

defend your spouse you will undoubtedly offend your in-laws; if you side with your in-laws, your spouse will feel betrayed. A better strategy is to let them work out their differences without becoming directly involved. If you are asked to take sides during an argument, you can say, *"I think it would be best if I stay out of this one;"* or *"I'm not in a position to make a judgment. I'd rather remain neutral."*

4. Most every parent feels a sense of loss when his or her child marries. For example, if your mother-in-law says, *"Now that my baby boy is married I guess he won't need his mother anymore,"* you can alleviate her fears by saying, *"Don't worry, he'll always need his mother!"*

5. Always remember your in-laws' birthdays, to send thank-you notes, and to make phone calls to say hello. This lets your in-laws know that you like and appreciate them. You can say, *"We really appreciate all the nice things you do for us. Thanks!"*

6. Be forgiving of critical in-laws. When a new person enters a family, he or she brings a new style and personality, which can be difficult for some people to cope with. You can say, *"We do things a little differently in my family, but will you show me your method?"*

7. Give your in-laws time to get to know you and accept your position in the family. Overprotective parents need extra time to trust and open up to new people, especially ones that may be seen as their replacements. You can say, *"I like your family very much and I'm happy that I am part of it."*

INTIMATE CONVERSATIONS MEAN YOU CARE

Telling a friend, spouse, lover, or family member what you honestly think is never easy, especially when there are sensitive feelings at stake or serious problems to address. Most people are not open with their feelings because they fear that they will be misunderstood or disapproved of, or cause conflict. However, breaking through the barriers to mutual understanding and respect is worth the risk because as you strip away the layers that separate superficial chitchat from intimate conversation you will become closer to the people you love. And after all, isn't that what intimacy is all about?